THE
RIGHTS OF
STUDENTS

THE AMERICAN CIVIL LIBERTIES UNION HANDBOOK SERIES

The Rights of Teachers
 by David Rubin

The Rights of Servicemen
 by Robert Rivkin

The Rights of Mental Patients
 by Bruce Ennis & Loren Siegel

The Rights of Prisoners
 by David Rudovsky

The Rights of Women
 by Susan C. Ross

The Rights of Students
 by Alan H. Levine with Eve Cary
 & Diane Divoky

The Rights of Suspects
 by Oliver Rosengart

The Rights of the Poor
 by Sylvia Law
 (with one chapter by Burt Neuborne)

AN AMERICAN
CIVIL LIBERTIES
UNION HANDBOOK

THE
RIGHTS OF
STUDENTS
THE BASIC ACLU
GUIDE TO A
STUDENT'S RIGHTS

Alan Levine
with EVE CARY
and DIANE DIVOKY

General Editors of this series:
Norman Dorsen, *General Counsel*
Aryeh Neier, *Executive Director*
Special Editor:
Ruth Bader Ginsburg, *Coordinator,*
 ACLU Women's Rights Project

7836

A Richard Baron Book
Sunrise Books, Inc. / E. P. Dutton & Co., Inc.

10   9   8   7   6   5   4   3   2

Published simultaneously in Canada by Clarke, Irwin & Company
Limited, Toronto and Vancouver

ISBN: 0-87690-137-2
Library of Congress Catalog Card Number: 73-84703

Contents

ALAN LEVINE is Director of the New York Civil Liberties Union Student Rights Project, the first full-time project in the United States devoted to securing the legal rights of students. Mr. Levine has represented large numbers of students in litigation and has written and lectured extensively on student rights.

EVE CARY is a staff attorney for the New York Civil Liberties Union. She was formerly a free-lance writer and editor of the Union's newsletter, *Civil Liberties in New York*.

DIANE DIVOKY was formerly on the Student Rights Project staff at the New York Civil Liberties Union. She is currently a senior editor of *Learning: The Magazine for Creative Teaching*.

Preface

This guide sets forth your rights under present law and offers suggestions on how you can protect your rights. It is one of a series of guidebooks published in cooperation with the American Civil Liberties Union on the rights of teachers, servicemen, mental patients, prisoners, students, criminal suspects, women, and the very poor.

The hope surrounding these publications is that Americans informed of their rights will be encouraged to exercise them. Through their exercise, rights are given life. If they are rarely used, they may be forgotten and violations may become routine.

This guide offers no assurances that your rights will be respected. The laws may change and, in some of the subjects covered in these pages, they change quite rapidly. An effort has been made to note those parts of the law where movement is taking place but it is not always possible to predict accurately when the law *will* change.

Even if the laws remain the same, interpretations of them by courts and administrative officials often vary. In a federal system such as ours, there is a built-in problem of the differences between state and federal law, not to speak of the confusion of the differences from state to state. In addition, there are wide variations in the ways in which particular courts and administrative officials will interpret the same law at any given moment.

If you encounter what you consider to be a specific abuse of your rights you should seek legal assistance. There are

11

a number of agencies that may help you, among them ACLU affiliate offices, but bear in mind that the ACLU is a limited-purpose organization. In many communities, there are federally funded legal service offices which provide assistance to poor persons who cannot afford the costs of legal representation. In general, the rights that the ACLU defends are freedom of inquiry and expression; due process of law; equal protection of the laws; and privacy. The authors in this series have discussed other rights in these books (even though they sometimes fall outside the ACLU's usual concern) in order to provide as much guidance as possible.

These books have been planned as guides for the people directly affected: therefore the question and answer format. In some of these areas there are more detailed works available for "experts." These guides seek to raise the largest issues and inform the non-specialist of the basic law on the subject. The authors of the books are themselves specialists who understand the need for information at "street level."

No attorney can be an expert in every part of the law. If you encounter a specific legal problem in an area discussed in one of these guidebooks, show the book to your attorney. Of course, he will not be able to rely *exclusively* on the guidebook to provide you with adequate representation. But if he hasn't had a great deal of experience in the specific area, the guidebook can provide some helpful suggestions on how to proceed.

Norman Dorsen, General Counsel
American Civil Liberties Union

Aryeh Neier, Executive Director
American Civil Liberties Union

Introduction

"Free the New York City 275,000" read a button worn by many young New Yorkers a year or two ago. The number was roughly the total of students enrolled in the City's high schools.

The condition of un-freedom which it described was not, however, unique to the schools of one city. According to the Carnegie Commission's comprehensive study of American public education, *Crisis in the Classroom*,[1] public schools across the country share a common characteristic, namely "preoccupation with order and control." The result is that students find themselves the victims of "oppressive and petty "rules which give their schools a repressive, almost prison-like atmosphere."

The rights described in this book grow out of the challenges initiated by students and parents to some of the practices which school administrators claim are necessary to "control" their schools. Courts today, however, frequently curb those practices, finding that they reflect the administrators' moral and political judgments about students' lives but have little to do with education.

The purpose of this book is to define the scope of school officials' power to regulate students' lives. The following chapters outline the law in specific areas, but they all reflect a common theme: School officials can make and enforce only reasonable rules of behavior that are directly related to the students' education. They do not have the

13

power to control whom you date or hang out with in school, or how you spend your free time. If you fall asleep in class because you were out all night at a party, you may be punished for sleeping, but not for partying.

School officials often try to justify their interference in the students' private lives on the grounds that they are empowered to act *in loco parentis*. In other words, they say that parents, simply by sending their children to school, delegate their power to control the children's conduct to school officials, who can then act in place of the parent.

Courts are becoming increasingly skeptical of this argument. For example, in a case involving corporal punishment of a student by a school official, a Louisiana judge stated:

> It might have been said, in days when schooling was a voluntary matter, that there was an implied delegation of such authority from the parent to the school and teacher selected by the parent. Such a voluntary educational system, like a system of apprenticeship . . . has long since disappeared. Parents no longer have the power to choose either the public school or the teacher in the public school. Without such power to choose, it can hardly be said that parents intend to delegate that authority to administer corporal punishment by the mere act of sending their child to school.[2]

The same reasoning applies to other rules and punishments for which the *in loco parentis* doctrine is given as a justification.

Some education officials are beginning to recognize this limitation on their authority. The Ohio Department of

Education, for example, has rejected the idea that schools may act in place of the parent.

> . . . To stand *in loco parentis*, one must assume the *full* duties, responsibilities and obligations of a parent toward a minor. School teachers and administrators obviously do not support the children in their care, nor do they provide most of the tangible and intangible necessities and securities that the child finds in his home. In fact, school authorities stand *in loco parentis* only to the degree that they may act somewhat like a parent does only some of the time for the purpose of maintaining order in the educational system. No one would saddle school authorities with the full duties of parents to care for their children until the end of minority. Thus it is misleading to term one narrow function of the school—that is, the disciplinary function—as being a function totally representative of the *in loco parentis* concept. *In loco parentis* should not, then, be the basis for defining parent-school relationships.[3]

The New York State Department of Education took the position simply that school officials have only the powers that have been expressly granted to them by the legislature, saying: "[T]he school and all its officers and employees stand *in loco parentis* only for the purpose of educating the child. The Education Law does not give the school authority beyond that."[4] In Delaware the Department of Public Instruction has issued guidelines on student conduct stating that "rules and regulations should not penalize the student for behavior not directly related to the educational responsibilities and functions of the school."[5]

More and more courts are saying the same thing. A Minnesota federal court made this comment about a boy's right to wear long hair in school: "Regulation of conduct by school authorities must bear a reasonable basis to the ordinary conduct of the school curriculum or to carrying out the responsibility of the school."[6]

These developments in the law of student rights represent a sharp break with the educational practices experienced by generations of American schoolchildren. Few of them ever thought to question the principal's word about what they could or could not do in school; and, if they did, they received little sympathy from the courts. But in the last few years, courts have begun to recognize that injustice in schools should be tolerated no more than in any place else in the society. The words of one federal court sum up this trend: "The Constitution does not stop at the public school doors like a puppy waiting for his master, but instead it follows the student through the corridors, into the classroom, and onto the athletic field."[7]

The single most important case in recent years setting forth the rights of students in public schools was decided by the Supreme Court in 1969: *Tinker v. Des Moines Independent Community School District*.[8] The decision is reproduced in the Appendix and should be carefully read.

Most of the cases discussed in this book involve high school students, although a few college cases are mentioned. Most courts now agree that "the relevant principles and rules apply generally to both high schools and universities."[9] The same should be true of elementary and junior high schools, although few cases have actually considered the rights of students at those grade levels.

Despite the developments in the law, you may still find that your principal continues to suspend students without hearings, keeps confidential records on students which parents are not permitted to see, and forbids student newspaper editors from printing satire on school policy because such criticism is "irresponsible journalism." Although those practices violate students' rights and would probably be declared illegal if challenged, rights do not have any effect merely because they exist in a lawbook. They are meaningful only if exercised.

When we say, for example, that a student has the right to go to school even though she is pregnant, we are aware that many schools still prevent pregnant girls from attending classes. That such a policy is illegal means nothing if it is not challenged.

Having said that, we should add a word of caution. Challenging practices that violate your rights can sometimes be costly. This may not make sense since the law says that persons may not be punished for exercising their rights. But, as a practical matter, although a principal may not be able to prevent you from handing out leaflets on school property, he may be less than enthusiastic when it comes to recommending you for jobs or college.

That risk, of course, is not very different from the one that citizens always run when they exercise rights contrary to the interests or desires of those who have power to affect their lives. Southern blacks won the right to send their children to integrated schools in 1954; those who attempted to exercise that right sometimes found that they could not find work or get credit from local stores.

If you choose to exercise any of the rights described in this book and you are penalized in any way, the local office of the ACLU or a lawyer might help. So might the support of your parents and your classmates.

NOTES

1. Silberman, *Crisis in the Classroom* (1970).
2. *Johnson v. Horace Mann Mutual Insurance Company*, 241 So.2d.588 (La. App., 1970).
3. *Rights and Responsibilities: Administrative Guidelines*, Division of Urban Education, Ohio Department of Education, Columbus, Ohio, 1971.
4. Formal Opinion of Counsel No. 91, 1 Ed. Dept. Rep. 800 (1959).
5. "Resource Material for Developing Local School District Policies Regarding Student Rights and Responsibilities," Delaware Department of Public Instruction, Dover, Delaware, approved Sept. 16, 1971.
6. *Westley v. Rossi*, 305 F. Supp. 706 (D.Minn. 1969).
7. *Dunham v. Pulsifer*, 312 F.Supp. 411 (D. Vt. 1970).
8. 393 U.S. 503 (1969).
9. *Scoville v. Board of Education of Joliet Township*, 425 F.2d 10 (7th Cir. 1970).

I

The Right To A Free
Public Education

Do you have a right to go to school?

Yes. All children in this country have both a right and,
except in Mississippi, an obligation to attend school for
about ten years. You are required by law to go to school
and, in turn, the state is required by law to provide you
with a free education.

During the past several years, there has been a growing public awareness that most people's chances to get a
good job and earn a good living depend on obtaining at
least a high school diploma. Courts have recognized that
the right to an education is fundamental and that the re-
moval of a student from school is a severe punishment,
which school officials have the right to administer only
in cases of serious wrongdoing and only with strict safeguards against arbitrariness and unfairness. This problem
will be discussed in a later chapter on due process.

There has also been some recognition that the right to
an education means the right to a good education—that
it means little to be able to attend a free school if you
still can't read when you graduate.

19

Law suits have recently been filed attacking the inadequate education provided in several school districts. A federal suit in New York City challenges the lack of special classes for Spanish-speaking students. The suit alleges that because these students receive inadequate English and Spanish language instruction, many are illiterate in both languages. Moreover, since all classes are conducted in English, the students are handicapped in every other subject as well.[1] A similar suit has been won in New Mexico.[2]

Another suit, filed in California state court, seeks to collect money damages for a student who graduated from a San Francisco high school with a fifth-grade reading ability.[3] The school district is charged with negligence in failing to provide the student with the basic skills of reading and writing, thus substantially limiting his future income. No decision has yet been reached in the case.

The federal courts first took up the issue of equal educational opportunity almost twenty years ago, when they held that schools may not be racially segregated. More recently the courts have begun to consider the legality of the unequal amounts of money available through local taxes for public education in rich and poor communities. Both of these problems are beyond the scope of this book.

Do children who are mentally or physically handicapped have the right to a free public education?

Yes. All children have this right. If a child is too handicapped to attend a regular school, it is the duty of the state to provide him or her with a special education. In response to one school district's argument that they lacked sufficient funds to provide special services for handicapped children, one court replied: "If sufficient funds are not available to finance all of the services and programs that are needed and desirable in the system, then the available funds must be expended equitably in such a manner that no child is entirely excluded from a publicly supported education consistent with his needs and ability to benefit therefrom."[4]

The court ordered the school board immediately to submit a plan showing how it would implement this order, whether through supportive services in regular schools, special schools, or tuition grants to enable handicapped students to attend special private schools. All children, the court stated, "regardless of any handicap or other disability, have a right to a publicly supported education suited to their needs."

Can a public school charge fees for educational materials such as textbooks?

Although many public schools do charge students fees for educational materials, some courts have ruled that the practice is inconsistent with the guarantee of a free public education found in most state constitutions.

The Supreme Court of Idaho, for example, in a case involving the withholding of transcripts from students who refused to pay a $25 annual fee, the proceeds of which went for textbooks and extracurricular activities, held that the fee constituted a charge for attending school in violation of the state constitutional guarantee of "a system of public, free common schools."[5] The court further ruled that it is never permissible for a school to charge a textbook fee since textbooks are "necessary elements of any school's activity. . . ."

In answer to the school board's contention that withholding the transcripts did not prevent students from receiving an education, the court stated that a transcript is a "necessary incident" of a high school education and that not only school attendance but "the entire product to be received from it by the student must be 'free.'"

The same reasoning would require a school to provide

pencils and other equipment that is necessary for participation in regular classes.

Can schools charge fees for participation in extracurricular activities?

In the Idaho case, the court said that fees might be required for participation in some extracurricular activities, but it did not discuss under what circumstances.

The Michigan Supreme Court, however, has formulated a test that distinguished between those activities for which fees could and could not be charged. The court said that no fees may be charged for anything that is "an integral, fundamental part of the elementary and secondary education."[6] The court included interscholastic athletics in this category, along with books, school supplies, and equipment, so the school could not charge students for materials used in courses such as photography, art, home economics, and industrial arts.

The Montana Supreme Court recently applied the same principle but worded the test somewhat differently: "Is a given course or activity reasonably related to a recognized academic and educational goal of the particular school system?"[7]

The Idaho and Michigan cases were cited by Wyoming's Attorney General in advising that state's board of education not to charge fees for any part of the regular public school curriculum.[8] He went on to state, however, that fees might be charged for extracurricular activities, although he added that school districts had an obligation to pay the fees for poor students who would not otherwise be able to participate.

Recently a federal court in Illinois reversed the decision of a lower court judge in a case involving fees for various graduation activities, such as a dinner dance and school year book. The plaintiffs, who were poor students, claimed that the state had the obligation to pay the fees for students who would be prevented from participating on account of poverty. The lower court held that students had no legally protected right to take part in these activities—that they were not an integral part of the right to an education—and dismissed the case. The higher court, however, reversed the decision and sent the case back to the lower court for a hearing on the issue.[9]

Although none of these decisions is binding on any other state, it seems likely that other courts will hold, on the basis of language in the various state constitutions describing public education as "free," that no fees may be charged in public schools for books and for necessary educational materials and even, perhaps, for extracurricular activities.

NOTES

1. *Aspira of New York, Inc.* v. *Board of Education of the City of New York,* 72 Civ. 4002. (S.D.N.Y.). In an opinion dated January 23, 1973, the court refused to dismiss the suit.
2. *Serna* v. *Portales Municipal Schools,* 351 F.Supp. 1259 (D.N.Mex. 1972). But see, *Lau* v. *Nichols,* No. 26155 (9th Cir. Jan. 8, 1973), *cert. granted,* June 11, 1973.
3. *Doe* v. *San Francisco Unified School District,* No.653 312 (Superior Ct.).
4. *Mills* v. *Board of Education of the District of Columbia,* 348 F.Supp. 866 (D. D.C. 1972). See also, *Wolf* v. *Utah,* Civil Action No. 182646 (Dist. Ct. Salt Lake City, Jan. 8, 1969).
5. *Paulson* v. *Minidoka County School District,* 93 Idaho 469, 463 P.2d 935 (1970).
6. *Bond* v. *Ann Arbor School District,* 383 Mich. 693, 178 N.W. 2d 484 (1970).
7. *Granger* v. *Cascade County School District,* 499 P.2d 780 (Mont. 1972).
8. Wyoming Attorney General, 1971 Opinion No. 4 (June 11, 1971).
9. *Williams* v *Page,* 309 F.Supp. 814 (N.D. Ill. 1970), *rev'd,* No. 18536, 6th Cir. (June 9, 1971).

II

First Amendment Rights

Perhaps the most important of all rights guaranteed in our society is the right to express one's opinions freely about problems and issues that affect our lives. That right is no less important for students than for adults. Most Americans between the ages of 6 and 18 spend nearly half their waking hours during most of the year in and around a school building. That is a large part of one's life, and the policies that govern the school have as much impact on students' lives as most policies formulated by the President and Congress have on the lives of adult citizens. It is as important, therefore, for students to be able to discuss school policies openly as for adults to be able to debate freely issues of national policy.

Of course, issues of national policy concern students, too, and they have a right to express their views on those questions as well. The war, the draft, abortion, women's rights, the environment, race relations, school busing, welfare, government corruption—these questions affect the lives of students directly, and they have the right to make their views known. If students have to wait until they graduate to do so, it may be too late for their opinions to have any impact. In the words of one Federal court: "It is incredible to us that in 1972 the First Amendment was deemed inapplicable . . . to high school students living at the threshold of voting and dying for their country."[1]

Do students have the right to express their opinions on any subject while they are in school?

Yes. The United States Supreme Court, in a major decision, *Tinker v. Des Moines Independent School District*,[2] held that students do not lose their right to free expression under the First Amendment to the Constitution when they enter school. The Court explicitly rejected the position taken by some school officials that, once inside the gates of the school, students may be prevented from expressing themselves—whether on school policies or national events—unless the school wishes to permit such expression. The Court said that, on the contrary, students may be prevented from expressing their views only when they (the students) "materially and substantially" disrupt the work and discipline of the school.

The *Tinker* decision is important to read (it is set out in full in the Appendix) because it is a clear-cut statement, applying to all schools in the country, of a student's right to constitutional guarantees in the school. The case involved students who were forbidden by school officials to wear black armbands in school to protest the war in Vietnam. The Supreme Court's decision does not merely protect armbands but is intended to apply generally to other means of expressing views. Other courts have applied the legal principles set forth in the *Tinker* decision to such forms of expression as newspapers, leaflets, buttons, and political clubs.

The *Tinker* decision is also significant because in it the Supreme Court recognized that the First Amendment right to free expression has an important place in our public schools. In other words, the First Amendment is not just to be grudgingly tolerated in school, it is fundamental to the American theory of education. As the Court pointed

out, "personal intercommunication among the students"—
on subjects that may not be officially approved—is as
much a part of the educational process as formal classroom teaching.

At this point we must once again warn that exercising
your First Amendment rights involves risks. School officials sometimes defy the law, and reasonable people can disagree in specific situations as to whether the expression of
views is "substantially disruptive." You may be acting
within your rights, but you also may have to go to court
to prove it. For example, despite the *Tinker* ruling, a Texas
school superintendent prohibited students from wearing
armbands on one of the Vietnam Moratorium days because he had heard that there were going to be disruptions at various schools. A court ultimately overruled the
superintendent because there was no evidence to support
his fears that the armbands themselves would cause the
disruptions,[3] but the students went through a hard fight.

If you're in doubt about the legality of a planned action, you may want to consider whether there are less risky
but still effective means of making your point. Ultimately,
you may want to consult a lawyer.

**Can students be prohibited from expressing their views
if those who hold opposing views become angry and
boisterous?**

No. Once *Tinker* established the test of material and
substantial disruption as a standard for First Amendment
activity, some courts were faced with situations where, although the students who expressed their views were per-
fectly orderly, those who took exception to those views
became threatening and disorderly. Quite reasonably, the
courts have consistently held that the rights of those who
peacefully express their views may not so easily be de-
feated. Thus, when school officials attempted to ban distribution of a student newspaper because of the hostility

of other students, the court said that if the student distributed the newspaper in an "orderly, non-disruptive manner, then he should not suffer if other students, who are lacking in self-control, tend to over-react thereby becoming a disruptive influence."[4] Perhaps where tensions at a school are very high, then regulation of "time, place, and manner" of expression of views might be permitted because of the fear of other students' reactions.[5] But "the administration should, of course, take all reasonable steps to control disturbances, however generated."[6]

Can students use school facilities such as bulletin boards, loudspeakers, mimeograph machines, and school assemblies to express their views?

If the use of these school facilities for expression of student views would not be likely to disrupt regular school activities, students should be able to use them. However, a school may legitimately refuse to allow students to use its mimeograph machine if, for example, it is used all day long in the preparation of course material. If the loudspeaker is used only for school business, such as the announcement of school activities, program changes, and special events, a court would probably hold that student groups may legally be prevented from using it for the expression of particular opinions. On the other hand, facilities such as bulletin boards should present no problem since space for the use of students can almost always be made available.

Of course, if any facility is made available to one group, the school may not then deny other groups the opportunity to use that facility.[7] A strong argument may also be made for the right of students to conduct an antiwar assembly if representatives from the military are permitted to defend the government's military policies. (The argument may not succeed.)

Can students wear buttons to express their views?

Usually yes, since wearing a button rarely disrupts any school activity.[8] However, one court refused to permit students to wear buttons because those handing out the buttons were being noisy and stopping other students in the hall.[9] In another case, students were not allowed to wear buttons because, in the past, students had worn racially inflammatory buttons that had caused tensions and disruptions at the school.[10] The latter two are unusual situations, however, and the school can almost never legally restrict the wearing of any button. The mere fact that someone finds the message on your button offensive is not a valid reason to keep you from wearing it.

Can school officials keep students from forming an after-school club having a dissident point of view?

No, unless the officials, applying the *Tinker* formula, can show that the club will "materially and substantially" disrupt school activities.

The right to form groups and associations has for years been recognized by the courts to be an important aspect of your right to express your views.[11] For example, forming a club in school might allow you to use various school facilities, such as bulletin boards, loudspeakers, and meeting rooms, or allow you to present a school assembly. One school had a policy barring clubs that expressed a "partisan" point of view and wouldn't give recognition to a high-school chapter of the Student Mobilization Committee. A court overruled the school administration, saying, as the Supreme Court did in *Tinker*, that the organization would make a substantial contribution to the educational process through the expression of its point of view.[12]

The Supreme Court has ruled in a similar case that a college could not deny official recognition to a chapter of SDS unless it could be shown that the aims of the chapter were to disrupt the school.[13]

Can the school prevent students from inviting a speaker to their club meeting because he is too controversial?

No. If clubs are allowed to meet and to decide upon their own programs, then they cannot be denied the right to invite a particular outside speaker because of his views, unless the school can show that the speech is likely to create disorder at the school.[14] The fear of disorder, moreover, must be founded on "clear and convincing" evidence and not on speculation based on the speaker's known radical views.

Can students be penalized for picketing outside the school, or for walking out of class, or sitting in, if the demonstration is peaceful and orderly?

The First Amendment protects "peaceable assembly," a provision generally applied to peaceful and orderly demonstrations. When it comes to demonstrations on school property, most court decisions have been unfavorable, particularly when the demonstration takes place during school hours or inside a school building. Under the *Tinker* test, it is more likely that such demonstrations will be found to "materially and substantially disrupt" school activities.

One court, for example, upheld the suspension of a group of black students who walked out of a school pep rally when the song "Dixie" was played.[15] School officials had found the walk-out disruptive. In another case, a federal court held that students could be suspended for staying out of school and conducting a rally to protest school policies that they claimed were racially discriminatory.[16] And still another court permitted a school to prohibit all demonstrations inside any school building.[17] Under *Tinker*, this decision seems clearly wrong because the lower court made no distinction between those demonstrations which did and did not disrupt school activities.

A Pennsylvania court analyzed the problem better. Even though it upheld suspensions for an in-school sit-in, the court stated that a sit-in was not illegal merely because it was indoors; or because other students gathered in the halls to watch; or because school administrators, who had chosen to keep watch on the demonstration, could not attend to their duties. The court said that in deciding under the *Tinker* test when a demonstration "materially" interferes with school activities, "the courts can only consider the conduct of the demonstrators and not the reaction of the audience."[18] The Pennsylvania court found, however, that this particular demonstration did materially interfere with school activities because the student demonstrators missed scheduled classes, and noise from the demonstration required some classes to be moved to different locations and disturbed others.

A demonstration outside the school building, such as a rally or picketing, has more chance of being found legal than one inside the building. The test, again, is material and substantial disruption of school activities. Thus a South Carolina court held that a school could not make a blanket rule banning all demonstrations on school property without regard to how orderly and peaceful they were. The court stated that under the First Amendment the school campus was a proper place for students to assemble for "peaceful expression of grievances" against school policies.[19]

From these cases it is clear that demonstrations during school hours run a greater risk of being held illegal than those held after school, for two reasons: (1) they are more likely to disrupt classes; and (2) many of the demonstrators will be illegally absent from classes. It goes without saying that your participation in any demonstration off campus, after school hours, is of no concern to school authorities.[20]

If you take part in a demonstration during school hours, miss classes, and consequently have your grades lowered, you might find out if other students who are truant generally suffer any penalty. If you are treated specially merely because your truancy resulted from a demonstration, the punishment may be illegal.

One final word: whether your demonstration is inside a building or out on the campus, a court is more likely to find the action legal if it concerns school policies rather than non-school issues. While a court may not be persuaded that a school is the proper place to protest against the war in Vietnam, it might recognize that it is the only effective place to protest against a long-hair regulation. In the words of the Supreme Court, "We would be ignoring reality if we did not recognize that the public schools in a community are important institutions and are often the focus of significant grievances."[21] You should be warned however, that anyone who demonstrates on school property runs a serious risk of being arrested.

Can a school prohibit students from handing out all literature, including underground newspapers, on school property?

No. This would violate the Supreme Court's decision in *Tinker*. Literature may be barred from school property only if its distribution materially and substantially interferes with school activities.[22] And even some disruption in handing out the literature does not justify banning the literature completely. As one court said, "It is their misconduct in the manner in which they distributed the paper which should have been stopped, not the idea of printing newspapers itself."[23]

That same court emphasized the point that minor disruptions could be tolerated to accommodate the right of students to express their views. Since the "interruption of class periods caused by the 'newspaper' were minor and relatively few in number," the court said, the *Tinker* standard of "material and substantial disruptions" had not been met. A word of advice: although a rule prohibiting all distribution of literature on school property is unconstitutional, you should ask school officials to change the rule before deciding to defy it.

Can students express their views by handing out leaflets in a classroom or in the halls or by setting up a literature table in the lobby?

Sometimes. Although the Supreme Court did not consider these specific means of expression in *Tinker*, it did establish the "material and substantial disruption" standard by which you should be able to determine whether your activities are protected by the First Amendment.

The words "material" and "substantial" are crucial because the Court recognized that *any* expression of opinion on a controversial issue may possibly upset some people. In the Court's own words, "any word spoken, in class, in the lunchroom, or on the campus, that deviates from the views of another person may start an argument or cause a disturbance." Such a minor disturbance or disruption, however, is no justification for prohibiting students from expressing their views.

Now, apply that test to the examples in the question:

(1) *Leaflets in the classroom.* Certainly not legally protected while class is in session and probably not before class either, since this activity would be likely to interfere with students' getting to their seats and preparing for class.

(2) *Leaflets in the halls.* Although this would not directly interfere with classes, you might substantially interfere with traffic in the halls and delay students from getting to class on time, especially in schools with narrow, crowded halls. A court applying the *Tinker* test might, therefore,

find such leafletting to be illegal. On the other hand, a blanket rule against handing out literature anywhere inside a school has been declared illegal by some courts, although school officials may make reasonable rules regarding the time and place of distribution.[24] However, a rule restricting distribution to a time and place that would prevent most students from getting the literature would not be reasonable. As one court said: "[B]y excluding the period when the vast majority of the desired audience will be present and available for communication, the restriction is in effect a prohibition. The First Amendment, includes the right to receive as well as to disseminate information."[25]

(3) *Setting up a literature table in the lobby.* If it's a small lobby and the table or students gathering around it clog up the lobby, you'd have the same problem as with the corridors. On the other hand, if it's a large lobby and there is no substantial interference with students' passing through, and you are not supposed to be in class or study period, a court would likely find that you had a right to set up the table. Your case would be stronger if you were able to show that the student government is allowed to have a table there to sell prom tickets or the parent-teacher association for a bake sale. After all, if their tables are not substantially disruptive, yours should not be either.

If a school official tries to stop you because students who take your literature are discarding it on the floor, you might suggest that he instead punish those persons for littering. That is how the law works where leaflets are being passed out in the street.[26] You should point out that if the school stopped you from handing out literature because other students threw it on the floor, it would be easy for those who disagree with you to take your literature and throw it around the school, and thus defeat your right to express your views.

May a school ban all literature on a given subject on the grounds that the subject is too controversial and may cause disruptions?

Some school boards seem to think that students may be prohibited from expressing their views on controversial issues as long as "both sides" are banned. Whether or not such policies are well intentioned, the *Tinker* decision no longer permits school officials to silence students because of the fear that controversy will disrupt the educational process. It is, in fact, the discussion of controversial issues, the Supreme Court said, which "is the basis of our national strength and of the independence and vigor of Americans who grow up and live in this relatively permissive, often disputatious society."[27]

In a Texas case,[28] where the school superintendent barred the wearing of armbands because of rumors of planned disruptions, the court warned school officials against basing their fear of disruption merely on "intuition" and gave this advice to school officials who too hastily prohibited students from expressing their views: "We believe that the Supreme Court [in *Tinker*] has declared a constitutional right which school authorities must nurture and protect, not extinguish, unless they find the circumstances allow them no practical alternative."

Recently, a school district barred a student from handing out and posting leaflets seeking volunteers for the "McGovern for President" campaign. The district claimed it had a policy·prohibiting the use of school facilities for all partisan political activities, a policy it applied against both major political parties. Nevertheless, a federal court ruled that this policy violated the student's First Amendment rights.[29] And another federal court declared unconstitutional a state law prohibiting distribution on school property of any material of a "sectarian, partisan or denominational character" or the purpose of which is to "spread propaganda."[30]

Can a principal require students to submit all literature to him for approval in advance of distribution?

No, unless there are clearly defined rules that describe the procedures by which prior approval must be obtained. Two federal appeals courts have even held that no prior approval at all can be required since such a rule would violate the First Amendment prohibition of censorship.[31] Courts that have allowed the requirement of prior approval of literature have demanded that the school board adopt specific procedural rules, such as one clearly stating which literature has to be submitted and to whom it has to be submitted.[32]

Most importantly, if prior approval is required, the school must set a definite and brief time within which a decision has to be made, so that the principal cannot indefinitely delay the distribution. A federal court in California, although approving in theory a policy requiring prior approval of literature, emphasized the need for a quick decision, warning that where the literature is "political or social, and the effectiveness of the item may be severely diminished by even a brief delay in its distribution, it may be that even one day's restraint is an impermissible burden."[33] If, for example, you have to submit to the dean for his approval a leaflet announcing a rally the next afternoon, you have a very strong argument for requesting a decision the same day.

Finally, the school may be required to provide an opportunity for the students to present their point of view at a hearing. If a decision disapproving their literature is made, students must have available to them "an expeditious review procedure of the decision of school authorities."[34]

It should be obvious, of course, in view of *Tinker*, that the school may not withhold approval of literature without evidence that its distribution will materially and substantially disrupt the school. Even without court orders, such arge urban school districts as Philadelphia and New York have decided on their own that it would not be proper to require students to submit literature for advance approval.[35] This policy is better because, among other reasons, it preserves the students' anonymity and thus prevents school officials from punishing those who distribute controversial literature.

Can students *sell* underground newspapers on-school grounds as long as there is no substantial disruption of school activities?

The one federal court that has ruled directly on this question said that students could not be barred from selling literature unless under the *Tinker* test there was evidence of disruption.[36] In two cases where courts broadly upheld the right to distribute underground newspapers on school property, the papers were either sold[37] or contributions were solicited.[38]

Can students solicit money on school grounds to support political and social causes?

Raising money to support causes in which one believes has long been held to be a protected activity under the First Amendment[39] and, therefore, the *Tinker* test of material and substantial disruption ought to apply to this kind of activity. The one court that directly considered the issue, however, denied students the right to distribute flyers soliciting funds for the defense of a political trial; the court feared that students might be subjected to pressure by various outside groups seeking to raise money for particular causes.[40]

If you want to solicit money in your school for a political or social cause, you should try to show that no serious problems would arise, such as substantial disruption of school activities or undue pressure being put upon students to contribute. One way you might show this is to give examples of other types of solicitations that are permitted by school authorities, such as various ticket sales, bake sales, sales of school publications, solicitations for charity, raising money for student government, sale of school rings, etc. For example, the New York Commissioner of Education has permitted a student council to sell candy in order to finance student activities.[41] If money may be solicited for these purposes, it is unfair, and maybe illegal, to prohibit students from soliciting money for other purposes.

May a student publication be banned because it criticizes a school rule and advises students to disobey it?

Once again, the starting point is the *Tinker* test of "material and substantial" disruption. To bar such a publication, school officials would have to be able to show that its distribution on school property would likely produce some serious disorder at the school.

In the major case on this question, students in an Illinois high school produced a newspaper urging their classmates to throw away some materials that were given them by the school staff to take to their parents. A federal appeals court said that the publication was protected by the First Amendment since there was no evidence from which school officials could reasonably have forecast a substanttial disruption of school activity.[42] In other words, the students were not rallying their classmates and preparing them for immediate action to disrupt the school.

Two other federal courts have taken the same position. One declared invalid a school regulation prohibiting any publication that advocates illegal action or disobedience to published rules on student conduct.[43] The other found unconstitutional a school board policy prohibiting distribution of any publication which "advocates illegal actions, or is grossly insulting to any group or individual.[44]

Can a publication be banned because it criticizes school officials?

No. Criticism of school policies and school officials is protected by the First Amendment. Some principals say that published criticism of school staff will undermine discipline among students. However, courts have not permitted such criticism to be suppressed if the school officials were unable to produce specific evidence that discipline would be substantially affected by the publication's distribution. One student publication suggested that a dean had a "sick mind," a remark that a court found "disrespectful and tasteless," but not justifying suppression of the publication under the *Tinker* test.[45]

Sometimes a school official will try to ban a critical article or publication because it is libelous. Libel is printing something that you know, or should know, is not true in an attempt to injure a person's reputation. If what you write is libelous, you can be sued for money damages. If your criticism concerns school policies, and you have good reason to believe that what you say is true, the statements will not constitute libel even if you are not able to prove they are true or even if what you write later turns out to be false. Nothing you say that is true is libelous.

If the school pays for a student-run newspaper, do school officials have total control over its contents?

No. Even though the school pays for the newspaper, school officials may not act as a censor of its contents if the newspaper has been a forum for the expression of student views. The principal may not prevent the publication of an article or editorial merely because it is critical of school policies or because he considers it too controversial.[46] In the words of one court, "The state is not necessarily the unfettered master of all it creates."[47]

This rule has been applied to a case where students attempted to place an antiwar advertisement in the school newspaper. Although the newspaper accepted commercial advertisements, the principal refused to permit publication of the ad because it did not relate to news of the high school. The court rejected this argument, noting that articles on the war had appeared in the paper and that the war was clearly a school-related issue.[48] Of significance is the fact that the court did not deny students this forum for communicating their views even though other modes of expression—such as conversation or armbands—existed for the students.

In another case, a court barred a school official from cutting off all funds to a campus newspaper because he disapproved of the newspaper's editorial content.[49]

Can a student publication be banned because the principal thinks particular words are obscene?

Probably not. "Obscenity" is a complex legal term that refers to the content of an entire writing, not the specific language used. When school officials say that a publication is obscene, they usually mean that it contains "dirty words." The mere use of dirty words is not illegal; still, you will avoid trouble if you leave these words out in the first place instead of having to fight the issue in court.

But if you think it necessary to use such words to be effective, or if you wish to distribute an already written article that contains them, you should point out that under recent United States Supreme Court decisions "obscenity" refers to literature about sex that meets three tests of illegality:

(1) predominantly appeals to prurient, shameful interests of minors:

(2) patently offends community standards regarding suitable sexual materials for minors;

(3) taken as a whole lacks serious literary, artistic, political or scientific value for minors.

To be illegal, it must meet all three tests.

Political and social literature and most other writings appearing in the student press meet *none* of these tests, even if they do use occasional profanities. You might remind school officials: "Critics of the established order have frequently found it necessary to use language that shocked their audiences—neither Ezekiel nor Martin Luther spoke in bland terms."[50] It would also be helpful to point out that many books and articles in the school library contain the same words to which the principal is objecting in the student literature.[51] One court, faced with such a situation, attacked the school officials for their "rank inconsistency," which the court found "arbitrary and unreasonable."[52]

A federal court in New York, in a case involving the censorship of a student publication because a story contained "four-letter words as part of the vocabulary of an adolescent and . . . a description of a movie scene where a couple 'fell into bed,'" held that student publications could not be banned as obscene unless they satisfied the three tests we mentioned. The court went on to state that "constitutionally permissible censorship based on obscenity must be premised on a rational finding of harmfulness to the group [to whom the material is directed or from whom it is withheld.]"[53] The dialogue was the kind "heard repeatedly by those who walk the streets of our cities, use public conveyances and deal with youth in an open manner." Because similar language appears in reputable books and magazines readily available to students, the language in the story could not be considered offensive to community standards for minors, and therefore should not have been censored.

Another New York court ordered the return of a batch of questionnaires on student attitudes concerning such subjects as sex and drugs. The literature had been handed out in school by students and subsequently confiscated by

school officials. The court held that while the questionnaires "inquire[d] into subjects which many may deem
unduly sensitive, personal or offensive, they do not fall
within the modern proscriptions of impermissible obscene
material."[54]

**Can students remain quietly seated during the flag salute
ceremony as a symbolic protest against the words of the
Pledge of Allegiance?**

Yes. On the basis of the principles we have discussed,
namely that peaceful and orderly protest is permissible if
it does not substantially disrupt school activities, every reported court decision on this issue has permitted students
to remain quietly seated during the flag salute to symbolize
their disagreement with the nation's policies or practices.
The major Supreme Court case dealing with the flag salute
was *West Virginia State Board of Education v. Barnette*,[55]
in which Jehovah's Witnesses won the right to refuse to
salute the flag. Although the claim in that case was for religious freedom, the court made clear that a compulsory
flag salute violated the right of all citizens to free expression,[56] quite apart from their religious convictions.[57]

The further question of the right to remain seated during the flag salute was raised by students in New York
City, who felt that the words to the Pledge of Allegiance
were not true in America today.[58] The school argued that
other students had followed the example of the original
students and were remaining seated, a consequence which
the court did not find disturbing. "The First Amendment
protects successful dissent as well as ineffective protest."
As to the fear of school officials that other students might
become "infuriated" at those who sat, the court said: "The
Constitution does not recognize fears of a disorderly reaction as ground for restricting peaceful expression." The
court held that, under the *Tinker* test, students had the

right to remain quietly seated during the flag salute as a matter of conscience.

The next year when some students in one of the same schools found themselves being harassed for remaining seated the court issued a further order stating that the students could not be required to obtain parental permission in order to remain seated.[59]

Two federal courts of appeals have reached similar conclusions and have upheld the right of students to remain quietly seated during the flag salute.[60]

Do school officials have the right to conduct religious exercises in school?

No. The Supreme Court has held that school prayers and ritual Bible readings, ceremonies which many schools hold at the beginning of classes each day, violate the students' First Amendment right to freedom of religion, even if the prayers are non-denominational and participation is voluntary.[61] Such ceremonies are illegal despite the fact that students may be excused from attending them.[62]

A variation of this problem is presented by "released time" programs which allow students to leave school for a period of time during the day for religious instruction. Such programs have been found constitutional by the courts as long as students are not pressured to participate and the educational program of non-participating students is not disrupted.[63]

Can a school require a student who has religious objections to participation in war and military training to take part in an ROTC or similar program?

No. A federal court recently held that a high school student who, by reason of religious training and belief, was constitutionally opposed to participating in military training could not be compelled, as a prerequisite for a diploma, to participate in a Reserve Officers Training Corps or other such program.[64]

NOTES

1. *Shanley* v. *Northeast Independent School District*, 462 F.2d 960 (5th Cir. 1972).
2. 393 U.S. 503 (1969).
3. *Butts* v. *Dallas Independent School District*, 436 F.2d 728 (5th Cir. 1971).
4. *Sullivan* v. *Houston Independent School District*, 307 F. Supp. 1328, (S.D. Tex. 1969).
5. *Guzick* v. *Drebus*, 431 F.2d 594 (6th Cir. 1970), *cert. denied*, 401 U.S. 948 (1971).
6. *Shanley* v. *Northeast Independent School District*, 462 F. 2d 960 (5th Cir. 1972).
7. *Bonner-Lyons* v. *School Committee of Boston*, No. 73-1150 (1st Cir. June 29, 1973); *National Socialist White People's Party* v. *Ringers*, 473 F.2d 1010 (4th Cir., 1973); *Zucker* v. *Panitz*, 299 F.Supp. 102 (S.D. N.Y. 1969); *Garvin* v. *Rosenau*, 455 F.2d 233 (6th Cir. 1972), *on remand*, Civil Action No. 36093 (E.D. Mich. 1972); *A.C.L.U.* v. *Radford College*, 315 F.Supp. 893 W.D. Va. 1970); *Kissinger* v. *New York City Transit Authority*, 274 F.Supp. 438 (S.D. N.Y 1967; *Wolin* v. *Port of New York Authority*, 392 F.2d 83 (2d. Cir. 1968), *cert. denied*, 393 U.S. 940 (1968).
8. *Burnside* v. *Byars*, 363 F.2d 744 (5th Cir. 1966).
9. *Blackwell* v. *Issaquena County Board of Education*, 363 F.2d 749 (5th Cir. 1966).
10. *Guzick* v. *Drebus*, 431 F.2d 594 (6th Cir. 1970), *cert. denied*, 401 U.S. 948 (1971).
11. *NAACP* v. *Button.*, 371 U.S. 415 (1963).
12. *Garvin* v. *Rosenau*, 455 F.2d 233 (6th Cir. 1972), *on remand*, Civil Action No. 36093 (E.D. Mich. 1972).
13. *Healy* v. *James*, 408 U.S. 169 (1972).
14. *Molpus* v. *Fortune*, 432 F.2d 916 (5th Cir. 1970); *Vail* v. *Board of Education of Portsmouth School District*, 354 F.Supp. 592 (D.N.H. 1973).
15. *Tate* v. *Board of Education of the Jonesboro (Arkansas) Special School District*, 453 F.2d 975 (8th Cir. 1972).
16. *Dunn* v. *Tyler Independent School District* 460 F.2d 137 (5th Cir. 1972).

17. *Sword v. Fox*, 446 F.2d 1091 (4th Cir. 1971).
18. *Gebert v. Hoffman*, 336 F.Supp. 694 (E.D.Pa. 1972).
19. *Hammond v. South Carolina State College*, 272 F.Supp. 947 (D. S.C. 1967).
20. *Shanley v. Northeast Independent School District*, 462 F.2d 960 (5th Cir. 1972).
21. *Grayned v. City of Rockford*, 408 U.S. 104 (1972).
22. *Eisner v. Stamford Board of Education*, 440 F.2d 803 (2d Cir. 1971); *Quarterman v. Byrd*, 453 F.2d 54 (4th Cir. 1971); *Shanley v. Northeast Independent School District*, 462 F.2d 960 (5th Cir. 1972); *Scoville v. Board of Education of Joliet Township*, 425 F.2d 10 (7th Cir. 1970).
23. *Sullivan v. Houston Independent School District*, 307 F. Supp. 1328 (S.D. Tex. 1969).
24. *Riseman v. School Committee of Quincy*, 439 F.2d 148 (1st Cir. 1971); *Sullivan v. Houston Independent School District*, 307 F.Supp. 1328 (S.D. Tex. 1969); *Hilly v. Cunningham*, No. 70-1528-C (D. Mass. Nov. 12, 1970).
25. *Rowe v. Campbell Union High School District*, Civil Action No. 51060 (N.D. Cal. Sept. 4, 1970) (3-judge court).
26. *Ibid.* See also, *Schneider v. Irvington*, 308 U.S. 147 (1939).
27. *Tinker v. Des Moines Independent School District*, 393 U.S. 503 (1969).
28. *Butts v. Dallas Independent School District*, 436 F.2d 728 (5th Cir. 1971).
29. *Sanders v. Martin*, 72C 1398 (E.D.N.Y. Nov. 21, 1972).
30. *Rowe v. Campbell Union High School District*, Civ. Action No. 51060 (N.D. Cal. Sept. 4, 1970) (3-judge court).
31. *Riseman v. School Committee of Quincy*, 439 F.2d 148 (1st Cir. 1971); *Fujishima v. Board of Education*, 460 F.2d 1355 (7th Cir. 1972). See also, *Poxon v. Board of Education*, No. S1894 (E.D. Cal. August 31, 1971).
32. *Eisner v. Stamford Board of Education*, 440 F.2d 803 (2d Cir. 1971); *Shanley v. Northeast Independent School District*, 462 F.2d 960 (5th Cir. 1972); *Quarterman v. Byrd*, 453 F.2d 54 (4th Cir. 1971).
33. *Rowe v. Campbell Union High School District*, Civil Action No. 51060 (N.D. Cal. 1971) (3-judge court).
34. *Shanley v. Northeast Independent School District*, 462 F.2d 960 (5th Cir. 1972).
35. Both school districts' policies are cited in *Sullivan v.*

Houston Independent School District, 307 F. Supp 1328 (S.D. Tex. 1969). See also, *Matter of Williams,* decision of the New York City Board of Education (March 30, 1971).

36. *Jacobs v. Board of School Commissioners of Indianapolis,* 349 F. Supp. 605 (S.D. Ind. 1972).

37. *Scoville v. Board of Education of Joliet Township,* 425 F.2d 10 (7th Cir. 1970).

38. *Sullivan v. Houston Independent School District,* 307 F.Supp. 1328 (S.D. Tex. 1969). In addition, the Commissioner of Education of New Jersey upheld the right of students to sell a newspaper inside the school building. *Burke v. Board of Education of Township of Livingston,* N.J. 1970 School Law Dec. 319.

39. *Murdock v. Pennsylvania,* 319 U.S. 105 (1943).

40. *Katz v. McAulay,* 438 F.2d 1058 (2d Cir. 1971).

41. *Matter of Darrall,* 5 Ed. Dept. Rep. 197 (1966). See also, *Jacobs v. Board of School Commissioners of Indianapolis,* 349 F.Supp. 605 (S.D. Ind. 1972).

42. *Scoville v. Board of Education of Joliet Township,* 425 F.2d. 10 (7th Cir. 1970).

43. *Molpus v. Fortune,* 432 F.2d 916, 311 F.Supp. 240 (N.D. Miss. 1970). See also, *Matter of Brociner,* 11 Ed. Dept. Rep. 204 (New York State Commissioner of Education 1972).

44. *Baughman v. Freienmuth,* No. 72-1892 (4th Cir. May 17, 1973).

45. *Scoville v. Board of Education of Joliet Township,* 425 F.2d 10 (7th Cir. 1970).

46. *Trujillo v. Love,* 322 F.Supp. 1266 (D. Colo. 1971); *Dickey v. Alabama State Board of Education,* 273 F.Supp. 613 (M.D. Ala. 1967); *Antonelli v. Hammond,* 308 F.Supp. 1329 (D. Mass. 1970).

47. *Trujillo v. Love,* 322 F.Supp. 1266 (D. Colo. 1971). See also, *Wesolek v. The Board of Trustees South Bend Community School Corp.,* Civ. No. 73 S 101 (S.D. Ind. May 25, 1973).

48. *Zucker v. Panitz,* 299 F.Supp. 102 (S.D.N.Y. 1969).

49. *Joyner v. Whiting,* No. 72-1630 (4th Cir. April 10, 1973).

50. *United States v. Head,* 317 F.Supp. 1138 (E.D. La. 1970).

51. *Keefe v. Geanakos,* 418 F.2d 359 (1st Cir. 1969).

52. *Vought v. Van Buren Public Schools,* 306 F.Supp. 1388 (E.D. Mich. 1969).

53. *Koppell v. Levine,* 347 F.Supp. 456 (E.D.N.Y. 1972).

See also, *Jacobs v. Board of School Commissioners of Indianapolis*, 349 F.Supp. 605 (S.D. Ind. 1972).

54. *Burford v. Board of Education of the Baldwin Public Schools*, Civil Action No. 8482/72 (Sup. Ct. Nassau County 1972).

55. *West Virginia State Board of Education v. Barnette*, 319 U.S. 624 (1943).

56. *Street v. New York*, 394 U.S. 576 (1969).

57. *State of Maryland v. Lundquist*, 278 A.2d 263 (Ct. App. Md. 1971).

58. *Frain v. Baron*, 307 F.Supp. 27 (E.D. N.Y. 1969).

59. The New York State Commissioner of Education has made the same ruling. *Matter of Bustin*, 10 Ed. Dept. Rep. 168 (1971).

60. *Banks v. Board of Public Instruction*, 314 F.Supp. 285 (S.D. Fla.), *aff'd*, 450 F.2d 1103 (5th Cir. 1971); *Goetz v. Ansell*, 477 F.2d 636 (2d Cir. April 19, 1973).

61. *Engel v. Vitale*, 370 U.S. 421 (1962).

62. *Abington School District v. Schempp*, 374 U.S. 203 (1963).

63. *Zorach v. Clauson*, 343 U.S. 306 (1952).

64. *Spence v. Bailey*, 465 F.2d 797 (6th Cir. 1972).

III

Personal Appearance

Can schools regulate the length of a student's hair?
This is the area of student rights about which the courts have been in the greatest disagreement. In the following states, school rules regulating the length of a student's hair are *unconstitutional* unless the school can show either under the *Tinker* test, that the hair length causes substantial disruption of school activities or that there is a rational relationship between the rule and a legitimate educational purpose:

> Arkansas, Connecticut, Delaware, Idaho, Illinois, Indiana, Iowa, Maine, Maryland, Massachusetts, Minnesota, Missouri, Nebraska, New Hampshire, New Jersey, New York, North Carolina, North Dakota, Pennsylvania, Rhode Island, South Carolina, South Dakota, Vermont, Virginia, West Virginia, and Wisconsin.

Schools are *permitted* to regulate hair length in the following states:

> Alabama, Alaska, Arizona, California, Colorado, Florida, Georgia, Hawaii, Kansas, Kentucky, Louisi-

47

ana, Michigan, Mississippi, Montana, Nevada, New
Mexico, Ohio, Oklahoma, Oregon, Tennessee, Texas,
Utah, Washington, and Wyoming.

It should be understood that courts having jurisdiction
over this second group of states have not *required* schools
to regulate the length of a student's hair. All they have
said is that students have no constitutional right to wear
their hair as they please and, therefore, the matter should
be left up to the school administrators to make whatever
rules they deem neecssary. If you live in one of these
states, you may still be able to convince your school to
abandon hair regulations. Washington, for example, is a
state in which long-hair regulations are permitted; yet the
Seattle school district rule on personal appearance is simply that a student's dress or hair style must pose no health
or safety violation and must not be disruptive.

The reasons most commonly advanced by school officials for regulating hair length are that it is distracting in
class to other students; that students with long hair tend
to be discipline problems and get lower grades than short-
haired students; that other students will assault long-haired
students; that long hair is unsanitary; that long hair is un-
safe in shop classes; and that students must learn to obey
rules simply because they are rules.

All of these contentions have been refuted by various
courts:

Distraction. A Texas court rejected the distraction argument, asking: "[A]re we really to believe that the appearance of a few long-haired males will topple the pillars of
the educational structure of our public schools? If so, then
fragile indeed is that structure."[1]

Another court stated that it had "the inescapable feel-
ing that long hair is simply not a source of significant

distraction and that school officials are often acting on the basis of personal distaste, amplified by an overzealous belief in the need for the regulations."[2]

Other courts have also recognized that styles change and that what may be distracting at one time isn't at another. A federal district judge in Boston put it this way:

> This Court takes judicial notice that hairstyles have altered from time to time throughout the ages. Samson's locks symbolically signified his virility. Many of the Founding Fathers of this country wore wigs. President Lincoln grew a beard at the suggestion of a juvenile female admirer. Chief Justice Hughes' beard furnished the model for the frieze over the portico of the Supreme Court of the United States proclaiming "equal justice under law." Today many of both the younger and the older generations have avoided the increased cost of barbering by allowing their locks or burnsides to grow to greater lengths than when a haircut cost a quarter of a dollar.

> Whether hairstyles be regarded as evidence of conformity or of individuality, they are one of the most visible examples of personality. This is what every woman has always known. And so have many men, without the aid of an anthropologist, behavioral scientist, psychiatrist, or practitioner of any of the fine arts or black arts.[3]

Grades. The connection between hair and grades was disputed by one federal court of appeals in these words:

> . . . The connection between long hair and the immemorial problems of misdirected student activism

and negativism, whether in behavior or in learning,
is difficult to see. No evidence has been presented
that hair is the cause, as distinguished from a possible peripheral consequence, of undesirable traits, or
that the school board, Delilah-like, can lop off these
characteristics with the locks. Accepting as true the
testimony that in St. Charles, Missouri, the longer the
student's hair, the lower his grade in mathematics,
it does not lead me to believe that shortening the
one will add to the other. . . .

The area of judicial notice is circumscribed, but I
cannot help but observe that the city employee who
collects my rubbish has shoulder-length hair. So do a
number of our nationally famous Boston Bruins.
Barrel tossing and puck chasing are honorable pur-
suits, not to be associated with effeteness on the one
hand, or aimlessness or indolence on the other. If
these activities be thought not of high intellectual
calibre, I turn to the recent successful candidates for
Rhodes Scholarships from my neighboring institution.
A number of these, according to their photographs,
wear hair that outdoes even the hockey players. It
is proverbial that these young men are chosen not
only for their scholastic attainments, but for their out-
standing character and accomplishments.[4]

Violence. In a widely quoted dissenting opinion, an appeals court judge from Texas rejected the idea that long-
haired students could be suspended because other students
might attack them:

"These boys . . . were barred because it was anticipated
that their fellow students in some instances would do things
that would disrupt the serenity or calm of the school. It

is these acts that should be prohibited, not expressions of individuality by the suspended students."[5]

It might be reasonable to suggest to school officials that they consider the teaching of tolerance to the short-haired students rather than punish those with long hair.

Sanitation and safety. Sanitation and safety arguments have been easily answered by several courts, which have pointed out that hair length and cleanliness are unrelated and that less drastic alternatives exist to making students get haircuts when long hair might cause a problem, as in a shop class or swimming pool. As one court said, "The school administration has failed to show why these particular problems cannot be solved by imposing less restrictive rules, such as requiring students to wear swimming caps or shop caps."[6]

Respect for rules. As for teaching respect for rules, one court stated: "Discipline for the sake of discipline and uniformity is indeed not compatible with the melting pot formula."[7] Another federal court expressed similar sentiments in holding a school hair-regulation unconstitutional: "[T]he constitutional premise is that from different tones come the best tune."[8]

Can schools regulate what students wear?

Wherever hair length can be regulated, dress can be regulated. Where the "disruption" test has been applied to hair regulations, it probably would also apply to dress codes. However, some courts that have permitted students to wear long hair have indicated that a dress code might not be illegal because, unlike hair length, clothes can be changed after school.[9]

Nevertheless, there seems to be no greater reason to

regulate dress than hair; and dress codes, like hair regulations, generally have more to do with the personal preferences of a school administrator than with education. As one court said in striking down a prohibition against the wearing of dungarees, "[T]he school board's power must be limited to that required by its function of administering public education."[10] The court said it had "difficulty accepting" the proposition advanced by the school principal that students who wore dress such as dungarees "become lax and indifferent."

In an early decision on this question, then New York Commissioner of Education James R. Allen, Jr. (later, United States Commissioner of Education) ruled that a girl who had worn slacks to school in violation of a school rule could not be barred from school.[11] The Commissioner conceded that the board had the power to make reasonable dress regulations relating to health and safety, such as prohibiting cleats on school floors or long-hair angora sweaters in a cooking class; but he held that the regulation against girls' wearing slacks was unreasonable and a violation of their constitutional rights.[12] For the same reason, Allen also declared illegal a prohibition against boys wearing boots.[13]

May students be forced to comply with a dress code or hair regulations adopted by the student body?

Where dress codes and hair regulations have been found illegal when promulgated by the school administration, they have also been found illegal when adopted by the student body[14]—on the grounds that a student's appearance is a matter of personal taste, which should no more be overruled by fellow classmates than by the principal.

Where, however, a dress code promulgated by the school was upheld, a code enacted by the student body was also upheld.[15]

May students be excluded from an athletic team because of the length of their hair?

Unless coaches can show that long hair interferes with athletic performance, there is no more reason to accept hair regulation as a condition for playing on a team than for going to school.[16] Vague fears about threats to discipline and team unity are not enough to justify a hair rule.[17] To quote a New York Commissioner of Education, neither team morale nor team discipline is "dependent upon uniformity by each member to a given hair style."[18]

May a school require students to wear a special gym outfit?

The right to a free public education guarantees that students do not have to purchase a particular outfit, but a school can require students to wear clothes that permit them to perform the required activities (for example, sneakers) and are not dangerous (e.g., no jewelry or large belt buckles). Guidelines established by the New York City Board of Education state specifically that schools may recommend but not require the purchase of a gym uniform and that students are to be graded on performance and not dress.[19]

NOTES

1. *Watson v. Thompson,* 321 F.Supp. 394 (E.D. Tex. 1971).
2. *Breen v. Kahl,* 296 F.Supp. 702 (W.D. Wis.) *aff'd,* 419 F.2d 1034 (7th Cir. 1969).
3. *Richards v. Thurston,* 304 F.Supp. 449 (D. Mass. 1969), *aff'd* 424 F.2d 1281 (1st Cir. 1970).
4. *Bishop v. Colaw,* 450 F.2d 1069 (8th Cir. 1971).
5. *Ferrell v. Dallas Independent School District,* 392 F.2d 697 (5th Cir. 1968).
6. *Bishop v. Colaw,* 450 F.2d 1069 (8th Cir. 1971).
7. *Breen v. Kahl,* 296 F.Supp. 702 (W.D. Wis.) *aff'd,* 419 F.2d 1034 (7th Cir. 1969).
8. *Richards v. Thurston,* 304 F.Supp. 449 (D. Mass. 1969), *aff'd,* 424 F.2d 1281 (1st Cir. 1970); *Massie v. Henry,* 455 F.2d 779 (4th Cir., 1972); *Mick v. Sullivan,* 476 F.2d 973 (4th Cir., 1973).
9. *Westley v. Rossi,* 305 F.Supp. 706 (D. Minn. 1969); *Dunham v. Pulsifer,* 312 F.Supp. 411 (D. Vt. 1970).
10. *Bannister v. Paradis,* 316 F. Supp. 185 (D. N.H. 1970).
11. *Matter of Dalrymple,* 5 Ed. Dept. Rep. 113 (1966).
12. The same rule was declared invalid by a New York State court: *Scott v. Board of Education, Union Free School District #17,* 305 N.Y.S. 2d 601 (S. Ct. 1969).
13. *Matter of McQuade,* 6 Ed. Dept. Rep. 37 (1966).
14. *Matter of Cossey,* 9 Ed. Dept. Rep. 11 (New York State Commissioner of Education, 1969); *Arnold v. Carpenter,* 459 F.2d 939 (7th Cir. 1972); *Bishop v. Colaw,* 450 F.2d 1069 (8th Cir. 1971); *Scott v. Board of Education,* 305 N.Y.S. 2d 601 (S. Ct. 1969).
15. *Mercer v. Lothamer,* 321 F.Supp. 335 (N. D. Ohio 1971).
16. *Long v. Zopp,* 476 F.2d 180 (4th Cir. 1973); *Matter of Myers,* 9 Ed. Dept. Rep. 8 (New York State Commissioner of Education, 1969).
17. *Dunham v. Pulsifer,* 312 F.Supp. 411 (D. Vt. 1970).
18. *Matter of Vartuli,* 10 Ed. Dept. Rep. 241 (1971).
19. "Guidelines Regarding Relationship of Pupil's Dress to Grading of Pupils in Physical Education," Bureau for Health and Physical Education, New York City Board of Education (December 23, 1970).

IV

Due Process

What does the right to "due process of law" mean?

The United States Constitution requires that government agencies treat all persons fairly. Specifically, the Fourteenth Amendment states that the government may not "deprive any person of life, liberty or property without due process of law." Your principal, your teachers, the coaches, school security guards, and all other employees of the school are employees of the government, and therefore under the Fourteenth Amendment have a legal duty to treat you fairly. This means that they may not impose any serious punishment for alleged misconduct without first having followed certain established procedures to determine whether or not you are in fact guilty.

Principals often say that schools are not courtrooms and that school officials must be able to enforce discipline without having to go through all the procedures of a criminal trial. What they ignore is that often the punishments imposed to "enforce discipline" can be as serious as those imposed on a person convicted of a crime. Expulsion from school and the consequent denial of a high school diploma, for example, might have a lifetime effect, depriving a student of a chance to go to college or to obtain many kinds of jobs.

Further, even if a punishment has no lasting consequences, due process should be observed for its own sake. As one court put it:

> Schools should be especially sensitive to their responsibility for treating students fairly. The American public school system, which has a basic responsibility for instilling in its students an appreciation of our democratic system, is a peculiarly appropriate place for the use of fundamentally fair procedures.[1]

Exactly which procedures may be required to determine a student's guilt or innocence of an offense and to impose punishment depends in large part on the seriousness of the charges and the possible consequences of conviction. At the least, you are entitled to know what you are accused of doing wrong and to the chance to tell your side of the story. In serious cases, this hearing should take place before an impartial person; and you might have the right to have a lawyer represent you, to call witnesses in your behalf, to question or cross-examine your accusers and the witnesses against you, and to have a transcript made of the proceedings for an appeal.

The right to due process also means that any punishment imposed must be in proportion to the offense committed. A serious punishment like expulsion should not be imposed for a minor infraction of the rules or for the kind of conduct for which other students in the past have received only mild punishment.

You should note that the right to due process is only half the battle in obtaining fair treatment in your school. A hearing only guarantees you a chance to show that you did not violate a school rule; it will not determine whether the rule was a fair one in the first place. If, for example, your school has a rule against holding hands in the hall, the right to a hearing won't protect you if you and a friend were in fact holding hands. Therefore, it is important to work for fair rules as well as fair procedures.

Who has the power to suspend a student?

In most states only a principal, superintendent, or school board can suspend a student, although some states allow a teacher to suspend, usually for a shorter period of time. If someone other than the principal suspends you, check the state law or school district by-laws; in most states the suspension is illegal. Sometimes a teacher will just tell you not to come to class any more but won't call it a suspension. Whatever it's called, not being allowed to go to class has the effect of a suspension, and you should request the same rights as you would have for a regular suspension.

Do students have a right to a hearing every time a teacher or principal wants to punish them?

No, only some of the time. The general rule is that a student has a right to a hearing for serious punishments, but not for minor ones. If a teacher makes a student sit in the back of the room for being noisy, there is no right to a hearing. But if the teacher reports the student to the principal and recommends suspension for the rest of the term, then the student is entitled to a hearing.

Keep in mind that when we speak of a "right to a

hearing," we are only speaking of what the law will *require* school officials to do. It may be that the law will require a hearing only when it involves a major disciplinary matter. That does not mean that your school should not be willing, in the interests of fairness, to give you a chance to be heard in any case in which you think you have been treated unjustly. Don't let the fact that you might not have a good court case keep you from insisting on fair treatment at all times.

Does a student have the right to a hearing any time he is suspended from school?

Rights regarding suspensions are generally set out in a state statute and sometimes in a school board regulation. Some schools have two kinds of hearings, depending on the length of the suspension. For suspensions of only a few days, the school may convene an informal conference at which student and parents meet with the principal to discuss the reasons for the suspension. Some school systems, such as New York City, allow you to bring an adviser. Ask for the right to bring one if you and your parents think you need help. The principal may call the hearing a "guidance conference," which, because it assumes you need guidance, also assumes you did what you're accused of. Whatever the conference is called, insist on your right to show that the suspension was unjustified. If a teacher or student has falsely accused you, ask that he or she be brought to the hearing. New York State, for one, guarantees parents the right to question an accuser about the incident. Longer suspensions require a more formal hearing with at least some of the due-process guarantees mentioned earlier (lawyer, witnesses, impartial hearing officer, etc.).

If your school attempts to suspend you for a long period of time without a hearing, the action is probably illegal. How long is "long"? One court compelled a hearing where the suspension was 10 days,[2] another for any suspension over 5 days,[3] and a third for any suspension over 2 days.[4] Some courts have ruled that, if the hearing will not be held for several days and the student will be suspended during that time, he is entitled at least to an informal, preliminary hearing, where he can perhaps show that he was wrongly accused or that suspension is not justified.[5]

If suspended, a student should show why the punishment is serious enough to require an immediate hearing: for example, that it will mean missing substantial work for the term, or possible loss of credit for a course, or missing an important school activity, or adversely affecting his chances of getting into college or getting a job. In the words of one federal appeals court, whether or not a suspension is serious enough to justify a hearing "should be judged by its effect on the student and not simply meted out by formula."[6] That same court subsequently warned school officials that when suspension hearings are required, they must be held promptly:

> [I]t may be that a student can be sent home without a hearing for a short period of time if the school is in the throes of violent upheaval. But even in such a case, a hearing would have to be held at the earliest opportunity.[7]

You should always try to get a hearing even if you have already been suspended for a few days and are back in school, because the suspension will be expunged from your record if you are found innocent.

Is a student entitled to a hearing before he can be transferred to another school for disciplinary reasons?

Probably, but before asking for a hearing, find out if the person threatening to transfer you even has that power. In many school districts only the superintendent of schools—not the principal—has the power to transfer students.

If you don't want to transfer, a court will probably require that you be given an opportunity for a hearing.[8] As we have said, courts compel hearings for serious punishments, and you can make a good argument that a transfer is likely to be as serious as a suspension: for example, the other school may not be as good academically, may not have athletic teams, may be farther from home, or may not have desired courses. One court recognized that a transfer was a serious punishment because it meant "the disruption of course content in the sense that continuity is unlikely to be attained upon forced transfer from one school to another."[9]

Can students be punished by being forbidden to participate in extracurricular activities without a hearing?

Courts have begun to recognize that extracurricular activities are generally a fundamental part of the school's educational program.[10] To be denied the opportunity to participate in these activities can be as serious a loss of the right to an education as a suspension. School officials know that prohibiting certain students from playing on a team or going on a class trip would be a more severe punishment than suspending them from school.

In support of your claim of a right to a hearing you could cite the opinion of a New York court[11] holding that a student who was charged with drinking a glass of beer in violation of the school's code of conduct for members of athletic teams could not be deprived of his varsity letters without a hearing.

What is the right to adequate notice of the charges?

Before you can be severely punished, you have a right to know the specific acts you are charged with committing. A hearing is useless if you have no idea what accusations you're supposed to be defending yourself against. This idea is one of the oldest in criminal law and is now becoming established in such administrative proceedings as school suspension hearings.

The typical letter from a principal to a student's parent says that his child is charged with "violating school rules" or "serious misconduct." Those phrases fail to give any idea of what offense has been committed or what rule has been violated. That is not adequate notice. A federal court in Washington, D.C., has required that the notice "state specific, clear and full reasons for the proposed action, including the specification of the alleged act upon which the disciplinary action is to be based and the reference to the regulation subsection under which such action is proposed."[12]

The New York City Board of Education has ruled that the terms "defiance of school authority" and "gross disorder" are not sufficiently specific to advise the student or parent adequately of the charges.[13] And the New York State Commissioner of Education has said that the notice of charges must be "sufficiently specific to advise the student and his counsel of the activities or incident which have given rise to the proceedings and which will form the basis for the hearing."[14]

In addition, courts have held that students have a right to know the charges sufficiently in advance of the hearing to permit them "to examine the charges, prepare a defense and gather evidence and witnesses."[15]

Can a student be punished for violating a rule he didn't know existed?

That depends in large part on whether he should have known of the rule's existence. Some school systems give students copies of the school rules. In New York City students receive copies when they enter school; in Des Moines, Iowa, they are mailed copies of the rules before the school year begins. In these places students cannot plead ignorance of the law. Furthermore, some courts have found no violation of due process rights when students have been punished for disobeying the command of a staff member or violating a school policy that students were generally aware of, even in the absence of written regulations.

However, the school may not punish you for violating a policy you had no reason to believe existed. If, for example, you sometimes leave school during a free period instead of going to study hall, and students have never been told of a rule or policy forbidding that, it would be illegal to punish you without a prior warning. On the other hand, if a teacher specifically tells you not to leave, and you do, it is likely that you can be punished even in the absence of a written rule.[16]

A variation of this problem is presented by the typical school rule that allows suspension for "misconduct" or "immoral or disreputable conduct," terms which give you little idea of what is prohibited. If you behave in a way which you reasonably think is permissible but a school official thinks is "misconduct" or "disreputable conduct," a suspension for that behavior would probably be illegal.[17] But if the principal warns you that certain acts are prohibited, don't rely on the absence of a written rule as the basis for defying him. Just disobeying a school official is grounds for suspension in most school districts.

Does a student have the right to an impartial hearing officer at a disciplinary hearing?

For serious punishments you have a right to a hearing before someone who was not involved in the incident and is not prejudiced against you. This will usually be members of the school board, but sometimes even they are too much involved in the matter to be fair judges of your case. When a Texas student was arrested on a drug charge and the school board discussed the matter with law enforcement officials before suspending him, a federal court ruled that the student was entitled to a hearing before the state commissioner of education.[18]

The New York Commissioner of Education has upheld this same principle, saying that a hearing could not be held before a school superintendent who had been involved at an earlier stage of the case.[19]

A court in Michigan has held that where serious punishment such as transfer was intended, a principal who witnessed the incident leading to the charges could not hear the case.[20]

To establish whether the person or board hearing your case may have prejudged it, you should ask for the right to question them about their previous knowledge of the incidents at issue.[21]

In the most favorable ruling yet handed down, the court required an impartial hearing officer in any case involving a suspension of more than 2 days. The court specified that the hearing officer not be an employee of the public school system.[22]

Does a student have the right to be represented by a lawyer at a disciplinary hearing?

Courts have held that students do have this right where serious consequences might result from a hearing.[23] A Washington, D.C. court has granted students the right to a lawyer at any hearing involving expulsion, suspension, transfer, or any other denial of access to regular instruction for more than two days.[24] In New York, state law entitles a student to a lawyer for any suspension over 5 days. This is also the rule in Philadelphia as a result of an agreement reached in a court case.[25]

Another example of consequences serious enough to warrant the right to a lawyer appears in a New York case. There the court ruled that a student had a right to a lawyer when, as a result of being accused of cheating on an examination, she was denied credit for the exam and was prohibited from taking other examinations.[26]

Since expulsion is the most serious punishment that can be inflicted by school officials, there is little doubt that a student is entitled to a lawyer at a hearing if threatened with expulsion.[27]

If the school has a lawyer to present charges against you, you almost certainly may have a lawyer to represent you.[28]

If there are not enough lawyers in your area to represent all the students who need help, you might try to get your parents and other adults to organize a service of non-lawyers trained in the law of student rights to help students in hearings and in other school matters. This has been done effectively in several parts of the country. No court has yet ruled on the right of an indigent student to be provided with a lawyer, but if you are threatened with serious punishment and cannot afford a lawyer you should certainly ask to be given one.

Do you have a right to bring witnesses to a disciplinary hearing?

Yes, if you are granted a hearing, you have the right to bring witnesses.[29]

Some courts have further ruled that you must be given the names of the witnesses whom the school will produce to testify against you,[30] as well as a report on the facts they will testify about.[31] The New Jersey Commissioner of Education requires that students be given any statements of witnesses before the hearing.[32]

The Chancellor of the New York City School System held that it was illegal for school officials to deny a student the right to produce a teacher to testify in his behalf by refusing to release the teacher from his duties or pay him for the time he spent at the hearing, since school officials were given time to testify against the student.

If releasing teachers from classroom duties to testify at your hearing is a problem in your case, you might suggest that the hearing be held after school hours.

Can the principal refuse to bring a student's accusers to the hearing because of the fear of retaliation against them?

The right to confront and question one's accusers is virtually absolute in criminal law, and the United States Supreme Court has extended this principle to welfare hearings.[33] The right is equally applicable to school suspensions and other administrative hearings.

School principals frequently suspend students on the basis of complaints from teachers or other students but refuse to give out the names of these complainants. That the accusers are afraid of retaliation may indeed be a genuine concern. However, the people who wrote the Constitution were even more concerned about the possibility of false charges against innocent persons by anonymous accusers motivated by personal feelings of malice or prejudice.

The problem arose in a recent New Jersey case involving two girls who had been assaulted by other students. Witnesses to the incident identified the attackers but requested that their names not be revealed because they were afraid of being beaten up themselves. At the hearing, the accused students claimed they were innocent, but they were not permitted to question their accusers. Their case went to the New Jersey Supreme Court, which ruled that in any suspension hearing a student had an absolute right to question his accusers.[34]

Recent federal court decisions have also upheld this right[35] and it is guaranteed by statute in some states.[36]

Whatever the law in your school district, you should always request the opportunity to confront your accusers. If you have been falsely accused by someone, questioning that person may be the only way you can establish your innocence.

Does a student have the right to remain silent at a disciplinary hearing?

The right to remain silent, that is, not to be required to testify against yourself, is guaranteed by the Fifth Amendment to the Constitution. You will rarely have occasion to claim this right, however, as you will almost always want to tell your side of the story. The most likely situation in which a student might want to remain silent is when he has had criminal charges brought against him for the same conduct that has led to the suspension. If the suspension hearing is held before the criminal trial, the student may want to remain silent because what he says about his conduct could be used against him in the criminal trial. Under these circumstances, a federal court has held that "one cannot be denied his Fifth Amendment right to remain silent merely because he is a student."[37] That means your refusal to testify at a disciplinary hearing cannot be used against you as an admission of guilt.

You should probably make such a decision only after consultation with a lawyer. If you and your lawyer think it is important for you to remain silent because of the criminal charges, you might ask that your hearing be postponed until after the criminal trial and that you be allowed to attend classes until the hearing.

What can students be suspended for?

The grounds for suspension vary from state to state, and often from school district to school district. They are usually set out in a state statute and sometimes in a school district by-law, and vary from "continued willful disobedience" or "open and persistent defiance of the authority of the teacher" in California to "insubordination" in New York to "refusal to conform to the reasonable rules of the school" in New Hampshire to "temper tantrums which disrupt a class" in Des Moines, Iowa. Most states make mere disobedience of an order by a principal or teacher grounds for suspension, although some, like California, require that disobedience be "continued." In those states, a single act of disobedience probably is not grounds for suspension.

If you want to know the precise, legal grounds for suspension in your school (and remember that these are the *only* reasons for which a suspension can be imposed), you should look in your state's education law and the by-laws of your school board. Your principal, school superintendent, or a school board member can probably tell you where to find these laws.

One final point: Courts have recognized that suspensions are an extreme measure that undermines the basic aim of a school system, namely to educate its students. When a student is barred from school by suspension, he is of course not being educated. Accordingly, suspensions should be used only as a last resort and only in an emergency, when there is no other alternative. Adhering to this principle, one court stated that a suspension was an administrative device to be used only to remove unruly students at a particularly tense time.[38]

Under this court's reasoning, suspensions should last only as long as the emergency continues. The kind of outbursts of anger that lead to most suspensions usually pass in a matter of minutes or hours. Under such circumstances, there is no reason for a suspension to last more than a day. The regular practice of suspending a student until a hearing several days later is an improper use of the suspension power. School officials have disciplinary powers only for the purpose of furthering education, and suspensions lasting longer than the immediate emergency serve no educational purpose.

A by-law and circular of the New York City Board of Education satisfies these principles.[39] First of all, it calls suspensions an "emergency" power. Second, it allows suspensions *only* when the student's behavior "prevents the orderly operation of the class or other school activities or presents a clear and present danger of physical injury to school personnel or students." Thus "disobedience" or "abusive language," without disruption or actual danger, is *not* grounds for suspension. Finally the suspension must be reviewed every day by the principal and may last only as long as the emergency lasts.[40]

A final protection was afforded to suspended students by a Washington, D.C. federal court: the student was to be provided with "alternative educational opportunities" during the suspension period.[41]

What can a student be expelled for?

Generally the power to expel students, *if it exists*, is found in state law. That law will usually say who has the power to expel; in some states (California, for example) only the school board has it. Many states do not permit school officials to expel students at all; that is, to bar them permanently from going to public school in the district. In fact, a permanent expulsion may well be illegal in almost all states in view of the right to an education guaranteed by their constitutions. Most states have laws saying that expulsion of a student can only last for a fixed period of time or until a certain condition occurs; for example, when the student's return is approved by a psychologist.

In any case the law generally does not permit any government official, such as a school principal, or agency, such as the school board, to impose any punishment he chooses on a student who breaks a rule. If you disrupt a class, and the principal tries to expel you, you might bring witnesses to testify at your hearing that other students received only short suspensions for such misconduct. If there is no good reason for giving you a punishment that is so much more severe than that imposed on other students (the fact that you had publicly criticized school policies in an underground newspaper would *not* be a good reason), then the expulsion is illegal.

Can school officials suspend a student to force his parents to come to school to discuss their child's record?

No. Some principals and guidance counselors have said that they have tried unsuccessfully to get parents to come to school to discuss their child's work or his attitude towards school. The student is finally either suspended outright or told not to return to school until his parents come in. This is absolutely illegal. A student can be suspended only for behavior for which the law prescribes suspension. No state's law makes a parent's failure to come to school grounds for suspending the child. As we said, suspensions are supposed to be for emergencies.

Can a student who is above the age of compulsory school attendance be discharged from school without due process?

The right to go to school lasts longer than the obligation. While you may not be *compelled* to attend school past the age of 16 or 17, you usually have a *right* to attend until you are 21 (check your state's law for the exact ages). Students above the compulsory attendance age have all of the same due process rights as younger students.

Is a student who is suspended from school for medical reasons entitled to a hearing?

Yes. Some principals try to avoid due process requirements by claiming that a disruptive student is psychologically disturbed and suspending him for medical reasons. Federal courts have said that a suspension on these grounds entitles a student to the same kind of hearing as any other suspension.[42]

Can school officials punish students for off-campus activity?

They shouldn't, because a student's off-campus activities rarely affect any legitimate interest of school officials.

A federal court in Massachusetts, however, upheld school officials who had placed three students on probation and excluded them from athletic teams for drinking beer off-campus before a school dance.[43]

A more just view of school regulation of students' private lives was expressed by a New Hampshire court, which held that a student who had come to school drunk could not be punished by suspension from school until she worked out the psychological problems between her and her parents. The court stated that while under certain circumstances suspension might be appropriate punishment for drunkenness at school, "[i]t is fundamentally unfair to keep a student out of school indefinitely because of difficulties between the student and her parents, unless those difficulties manifest themselves in a real threat to school discipline."[44] In other words, the school had no business interfering with a student's problems at home, although it did have the right to punish a student for misconduct in school that might be the result of those problems.

A New York student who criticized his high school principal on a radio program went to court when he found that a report of his comments had been placed in his school record. The court ordered the report to be expunged and went on to say: "It is almost inconceivable that in this enlightened day and age a professional administrator could permit the entry in the record of a student of an item which is not only irrelevant but also obviously unconstitutional."[45] Again the court was saying that what a student does or says off-campus is of no concern to his school's administrators.

A New Jersey court has held that a student may be temporarily suspended for his off-campus acts only if those acts give school officials "reasonable cause to believe that

a student . . . presents a danger to himself, to others or
to school property."[46] Even that action, the court stated,
could be taken only after a hearing.

A federal court in Texas, in a case involving off-
campus distribution of an underground newspaper, stated:

> [I]t makes little sense to extend the influence of
> school administration to off-campus activity under
> the theory that such activity might interfere with the
> function of education. School officials may not judge
> a student's behavior while he is in his home with
> his family nor does it seem to this court that they
> should have jurisdiction over his acts on a public
> street corner. . . .
> Arguably, misconduct by students during non-school
> hours and away from school premises could, in cer-
> tain situations have such a lasting effect on other
> students that disruption could result during the next
> school day. Perhaps then administrators should be
> able to exercise some degree of influence over off-
> campus conduct. This court considers this power to
> be questionable.[47]

Today many schools are deciding on their own that a
student's off-campus activities are no concern of theirs.
For example, the Greensboro, North Carolina, Board of
Education restricts its rules against weapons and drugs to
"school premises" and "any school activity, function or
event."

On the other hand commission of serious criminal acts,
including narcotics offenses, has been held to be cause
for suspension from school even though the activity took
place off campus. A federal court in Texas, for example,

upheld a school policy of expelling any student for the rest of the school year for "using, selling, or possessing a dangerous drug" (including marijuana.)[48] The court's decision, we believe, represents an unnecessary extension of the responsibility of school officials for off-school activities. Although a principal may be concerned about drug use and wish to warn students about its dangers, it is difficult to accept the position that mere possession of marijuana off-campus, especially in these times, makes a student a threat to his classmates.

Can a student be suspended for being arrested even if he has not yet been convicted?

"One of the most basic concepts of American justice is that [a person] be deemed to be innocent until proven guilty."[49]

Since an arrest is only an accusation and not a conviction, the Commissioners of Education in both New York and New Jersey have ruled that suspension on the basis of an arrest alone is illegal.[50]

A school may hold a suspension hearing to try to prove that you actually committed the offense for which you were arrested. If the evidence proves that you committed the offense, and the offense is one related to school activities, you probably can be suspended even before your court trial. You should consult a lawyer before going to a school hearing that precedes a court appearance; as we said before, what you say at the first hearing can be used against you at the second.

Does a student have the right to appeal the decision to suspend?

Most school districts permit an appeal after the principal's suspension hearing, and one federal court has guaranteed the right to an appeal.[51] The appeal usually goes to the superintendent and then to the school board. In some states, the student has a right to a further appeal to the state commissioner or superintendent of education. The letter advising you of your suspension should provide information about how to appeal; but if it does not, you can probably get the information from the school board office or the state department of education. If there are no procedures for appealing, you might try to get a court to overrule the suspension.

To appeal a suspension, it is important to have a written decision that discusses the testimony and states the reason for imposing the suspension; otherwise, the person reviewing the case or appeal cannot determine whether there was a legal basis for the suspension. A written decision with a statement of reasons has been required by some federal courts and by the New York Commissioner of Education.[52] Where a hearing is held on a long-term suspension or on an expulsion, you should have a right to a tape recording or transcript of the hearing.[53] This requirement is made in New York for any suspension over 5 days. A Florida court ruled that a written memorandum of findings of fact must be filed by school officials after a hearing, declaring that the mere conclusion of "guilty of the misconduct as charged" was insufficient to permit adequate review.[54]

NOTES

1. *Lucia v. Duggan*, 303 F.Supp. 112 (D. Mass., 1969).
2. *Black Students of North Fort Myers Jr.-Sr. High School v. Williams*, 470 F.2d 957 (5th Cir. 1972).
3. *Vail v. Board of Education of Portsmouth School District*, 354 F.Supp. 592 (D.N.H. 1972).
4. *Mills v. Board of Education of the District of Columbia*, 348 F.Supp. 866 (D.D.C. 1972).
5. *R.R. v. Board of Education*, 109 N.J. Super. 337, 263 A.2d 180 (1970); *Stricklin v. Regents of University of Wisconsin*, 297 F.Supp. 416 (W.D. Wis. 1969); *Vail v. Board of Education of Portsmouth School District*, 354 F.Supp. 592 (D.N.H. 1972).
6. *Shanley v. Northeast Independent School District*, 462 F.2d 960 (5th Cir. 1972).
7. *Pervis v. LaMarque Independent School District*, 466 F.2d 1054 (5th Cir. 1972).
8. *Carson v. Board of School Directors of Milwaukee*, Civil Action No. 72-C-284 (E. D. Wis. Sept. 8, 1972); *Owen v. Devlin*, Civil Action No. 69-118-G (D. Mass. 1969); *Cardwell v. Albany Unified School District*, Civil Action No. C-70 1893 WTS (N. D. Cal. 1970); *Mills v. Board of Education of the District of Columbia*, 348 F.Supp. 866 (D.DC. 1972) *Betts v. Board of Education of Chicago*, 466 F.2d 629 (7th Cir. 1972).
9. *Detroit Board of Education v. Scott*, Civil Action No. 176-814 (Cir. Ct. Mich. 1972).
10. *Moran v. School District #7, Yellowstone County*, 350 F.Supp. 1180 (D. Mont. 1972); *Kelley v. Metropolitan County Board of Education*, 293 F.Supp. 485 (M.D. Tenn. 1968); *Matter of Myers*, 9 Ed. Dept. Rep. 8 (New York State Commissioner of Education, 1969).
11. *O'Connor v. Board of Education of School District No. 1;* 316 N.Y.S.2d 799 (S.Ct. 1970).
12. *Mills v. Board of Education of the District of Columbia*, 348 F.Supp. 866 (D.D.C. 1972).
13. *Matter of Castelli*, New York City Board of Education (May 28, 1970).

14. *Matter of Rose,* 10 Ed. Dept. Rep. 4 (1970).
15. *Sullivan v. Houston Independent School District,* 307 F.Supp. 1328 (S.D. Tex. 1969); *Fielder v. Board of Education of School District of Winnebago (Nebraska),* 346 F.Supp. 722 (D. Neb. 1972); *Caldwell v. Cannady,* Civil Action No. CA-5-994 (N.D. Tex. Jan. 27, 1972); *Esteban v. Central Missouri State College,* 277 F.Supp. 649 (W.D. Mo. 1967).
16. *Melton v. Young,* 328 F.Supp. 88 (E.D. Tenn. 1971), aff'd, 465 F.2d 1332 (6th Cir. 1972).
17. *Soglin v. Kauffman,* 295 F.Supp. 978, aff'd, 418 F.2d 163 (7th Cir. 1969); *Sullivan v. Houston Independent School District,* 307 F.Supp. 1328 (S.D. Tex. 1969).
18. *Caldwell v. Cannady,* Civil Action No. CA-5-994 (N.D. Tex. Jan. 27, 1972). See also, *French v. Bashful,* C.A. 70-243 (E.D. La. Feb. 17, 1970).
19. *Matter of Dishaw,* 10 Ed. Dept. Rep. 34 (1970).
20. *Detroit Bd. of Education v. Scott,* Civ. Action No. 176-814 (Cir. Ct. Mich. Jan. 12, 1972); see also, *Murray v. West Baton Rouge Parish School Board,* 472 F.2d 438 (5th Cir. Jan. 19, 1973).
21. *Wasson v. Trowbridge,* 382 F.2d 807 (2d Cir. 1967).
22. *Mills v. Board of Education of the District of Columbia,* 348 F.Supp. 866 (D.D.C. 1972).
    In its "Guidelines to School Districts Relating to Student-Board Rights and Responsibilities" adopted March 5, 1970, the Washington State Board of Education suggests that hearings be held before "an impartial hearing individual or board—not one involved in the alleged infraction or one biased prior to the hearing."
23. *Givens v. Poe* 346 F.Supp. 202 (D.N.C. 1972); *Goldwyn v. Allen,* 281 N.Y.S.2d 899 (Sup. Ct. 1967).
24. *Mills v. Board of Education of the District of Columbia,* 348 F.Supp. 866 (D.D.C. 1972).
25. *Jones v. Gillespie,* Civil Action No. 4198 (Ct. of Common Pleas, Phila. April 22, 1970).
26. *Goldwyn v. Allen,* 281 N.Y.S.2d 899 (Sup. Ct. 1967).
27. *Madera v. Board of Education of the City of New York,* 386 F.2d 778 (2d Cir. 1967).
28. *Hopkins v. Ayres,* Civil Action No. WC 6974-S (N.D. Miss. Dec. 9, 1969); *French v. Bashful,* 303 F.Supp. 1333 (E.D. La. 1969).
29. *Mills v. Board of Education of the District of Columbia,*

348 F.Supp. 866 (D.D.C. 1972); *Givens v. Poe,* 346 F. Supp. 202 (D.N.C. 1972).

30. *Hobson v. Bailey,* 309 F.Supp. 1393 (W.D. Tenn. 1970).
31. *Caldwell v. Cannady,* Civil Action No. CA-5-994 (N.D. Tex. Jan. 27, 1972).
32. *Scher v. Board of Education of West Orange,* 1969 School Law Dec. 92.
33. *Goldberg v. Kelly,* 397 U.S. 254 (1970).
34. *Tibbs v. Board of Education of the Township of Franklin,* 59 N.J. 506, 284 A.2d 179 (1971).
35. *Mills v. Board of Education of the District of Columbia,* 348 F.Supp. 866 (D.D.C. 1972); *Fielder v. Board of Education of School District of Winnebago (Nebraska),* 346 F.Supp. 722 (D. Neb. 1972); *De Jesus v. Penberthy,* 344 F.Supp. 70 (D. Conn. 1972); *Givens v. Poe,* 346 F. Supp. 202 (D.N.C. 1972).
36. See, *e.g.,* Sec. 3214(3) New York State Education Law.
37. *Caldwell v. Cannady,* Civil Actions No. 5-994, 5-1001, and 5-1002 (N. D. Tex. Mar. 9, 1972).
38. *Williams v. Dade County School Board,* 441 F.2d 299 (5th Cir. 1971).
39. Section 90, subdivision 42, By-laws and Special Circular No. 103 (1969-1970), of the Board of Education of the City of New York.
40. Another circular expresses the hope that a "resolution might be effected on the first or second day." Asst. Supt. Circular No. 10 (1967-68).
41. *Mills v. Board of Education of the District of Columbia,* 348 F.Supp. 866 (D.D.C. 1972).
42. *Mills v. Board of Education of the District of Columbia,* 348 F.Supp. 866 (D.D.C. 1972); *Marlega v. Board of School Directors.* Civil Action No. 70-C-8 U.S.D.C. (E.D. Wisc. Sept. 18, 1970).
43. *Hasson v. Boothby,* 318 F.Supp. 1183 (D. Mass. 1970).
44. *Cook v. Edwards,* 341 F.Supp. 307 (D. N. H. 1972).
45. *Matter of Shakin v. Schuker,* Index No. 6312/71 (Sup. Ct., Queens Co. Nov. 16, 1971).
46. *R.R. v. Board of Education,* 109 N.J. Super. 337, 263 A.2d 180 (1970).
47. *Sullivan v. Houston Independent School District,* 307 F.Supp. 1328 (S.D. Tex. 1969).
48. *Caldwell v. Cannady,* Civil Action No. 5-994, 5-1001, 5-1002 (N.D. Tex. March 9, 1972).
49. *Matter of Rodriguez,* 8 Ed. Dept. Rep. 214 (1969).

50. *Matter of Rodriguez, supra; Diggs v. Board of Education of Camden,* 1970 Schl. L. Dec. 225. See also, *Howard v. Clark,* 299 N.Y.S.2d 65 (Supt. Ct. 1969) in which the court found that arrest was not one of the grounds set out for suspension in state law.
51. *Mills v. Board of Education of the District of Columbia,* 348 F.Supp. 866 (D.D.C. 1972).
52. *Hopkins v. Ayres,* Civil Action No. WC 6974-S (N.D. Miss. Oct. 24, 1969); *Due v. Florida A&M University,* 233 F.Supp, 396 (N.D. Fla. 1963); *Matter of Rose,* 10 Ed. Dept. Rep. 4 (1970); *Esteban v. Central Missouri State College,* 277 F.Supp. 649 (W.D. Mo. 1967).
53. *Matter of Rose,* 10 Ed. Dept. Rep. 4 (1970); *Givens v. Poe,* 346 F.Supp. 202 (D.N.C. 1972).
54. *Veasey v. Board of Public Instruction,* 247 So.2d 80 (Dist. Ct. App. Fla. 1971).

V

Law Enforcement

The fear of drugs and violence and student discontent has led many schools to hire policemen or security guards, sometimes dressed as students, and to introduce into the school routine various "security" measures, such as I.D. cards with photographs or electronic surveillance systems.

These measures may or may not keep order, but what they often do accomplish is the destruction of an atmosphere conducive to learning. Once a school reaches the point where students are being watched by surveillance devices, fingerprinted for identification, eavesdropped in class by undercover police agents, or confronted in the halls by security guards, education becomes difficult if not impossible.

May school officials require students to submit to questioning by the police?

Neither school officials nor anybody else can make students talk to the police. You have a constitutional right to remain silent. The practice in some schools is for school officials to cooperate with police investigations by taking students from class and making them available for questioning. In New York, the State Education Department has warned school boards "that children are given over to the custody of the school authorities for one purpose only and that is education in all its phases."[1] Therefore, "police authorities have no power to interview children in the school building or to use the school facilities in connection with police-department work, and the board has no right to make children available for such purposes." Police who wish to speak to a student must take the matter up directly with the student's parents.

Most other states have no official policy regarding police interviews of students in school. The Delaware Department of Public Instruction did the next best thing to prohibiting such interviews by establishing guidelines to govern them. These are:

a. The parent should be notified of the request before the questioning whenever possible.

b. The student should be apprised of the reasons for the questioning and of his legal rights.

e. The principal or his designated representative should be present during the questioning session.

d. The procedural aspects of due process should be observed.[2]

What should a student do to protect himself in interviews with the police?

You have a right to remain silent, and this is probably the best course to take. You should give the police your name and address. If they don't know who you are, they may be more likely to arrest you since they won't be able to get in touch with you any other way. But, until you have spoken to your parents or a lawyer, don't answer any questions—even if the school authorities say it is in your best interest to do so, or even if the police have said you will not be allowed to leave until you have answered their questions.

There are occasions when nothing bad would come of answering a few questions on the spot to clear up a simple misunderstanding; you must use your own judgment. You should keep in mind, however, that it is the job of the police to investigate crimes. If you have any reason to believe that you are suspected of committing a crime, don't explain, don't lie, don't confess. *Don't* talk, except to ask to call your parents or a lawyer. It's far better to err on the side of caution and not answer questions. You can't get into trouble by remaining silent; but if you talk, what you say may be used against you.

Can police or school officials search a student's desk or locker?

One thing should be said on this subject before anything else: Do not put anything in your desk or locker that you would not want the police or school officials to know about. The law allows students' lockers to be searched, despite the Fourth Amendment's prohibition against "unreasonable searches and seizures" of persons, their homes and private belongings. For a search to be legal in the outside world, the government official must generally have a search warrant signed by a judge or the express consent of the person whose property is to be searched. No court, however, has yet chosen to apply these specific constitutional protections to a high school student's locker or desk or other place *in school* in which he keeps his personal things.

There will be a lot of litigation in the area of school-locker searches, which we hope will bring changes. In the meantime, assume that your desk locker may be searched.

The leading case in this area concerned a New York student, whose locker was searched by police upon the permission of a vice-principal. Four marijuana cigarettes were found in the locker. The court held that since the vice-principal assigned the lockers to the students and possessed a master key, he had the authority to consent to the search of the locker because it remained under the school's control.[3]

"Indeed, it is doubtful if a school would be properly discharging its duty of supervision over the students, if it failed to retain control over the lockers," the judges concluded. "Not only have the school authorities a right to inspect, but this right becomes a duty when suspicion arises that something of any illegal nature may be secreted there."

In a similar case, and for much the same reasons, the Kansas Supreme Court decided that a high school principal may open a student's locker for the police without a search warrant.[4]

A California court also held that a high-school official could search the locker of a student suspected of selling methedrine to his classmates.[5]

There is much to criticize in the reasoning of all of these decisions, and the courts may someday move toward greater respect for the right of students to be free from unconstitutional searches.[6] Perhaps it is understandable that school officials, responding to the public outcry against drugs and violence in the schools, are tempted to use any means necessary to eliminate these problems. Yet it may be useful to remind these officials over and over again that abandoning constitutional protections is, in the long run, a dangerous policy. As the Supreme Court has said:

> That [schools] are educating the young for citizenship is reason for scrupulous protection of Constitutional freedoms of the individual if we are not to strangle the free mind at its source and teach youth to discount important principles of our government as mere platitudes.[7]

Can a school official or policeman search a student's person?

The Fourth Amendment protects citizens against searches of their persons as well as of their property, but a public school student has almost as little protection against the search of his person as against the search of his locker or desk.

This wasn't always so. In 1930 a Tennessee court, in a suit brought by a student who had been searched by one teacher at the request of another who suspected him of stealing money from her purse, held that the teacher's search was beyond her authority because it had nothing to do with the "educational process".[8] The court noted that a "child in the public schools . . . is entitled to as much protection as a bootlegger."

More recent cases have not been as favorable. The New York State Court of Appeals rendered a disastrous decision, *People* v. *Jackson,* upholding the search of a student by a school official and a policeman, who had pursued and caught the boy off school grounds after seeing a suspicious bulge in his pocket. The court held that the school official had "reasonable grounds for suspecting that something unlawful was being committed or about to be committed" and that this was sufficient to justify the search in view of the "distinct relationship" (*in loco parentis*) of the school official to his student.[9] Two other decisions have, on similar grounds, upheld the right of school officials to search students' persons.[10]

These opinions not only distort the Fourth Amendment search and seizure law but also the recent law concerning the *in loco parentis* doctrine. For one thing, as the ACLU brief in the *Jackson* case pointed out:

> By no stretch of logic or imagination can it be reasoned that the parents of André Jackson delegated to the school dean the power to chase their son off school grounds, search him, and initiate proceedings against him which might result in a prison term.

Further, not only the law but the logic is faulty in these cases; for if a principal were really acting *in loco parentis*, he would have a duty to be more, rather than less, solicitous of a student's constitutional rights. The *in loco parentis* doctrine is not a justification for overriding constitutional rights because a parent does not have the right to surrender his child's rights.[11] As a decision more than a half century ago stated:[12]

> Reasonable rules to enforce discipline, to preserve order, both in the school building and upon the grounds, to protect the morals, the health, and the safety of pupils, and to do, and to require pupils to do, whatever is reasonably necessary to preserve and conserve all of these interests may be made and

enforced. But any such rule or regulation . . . must be reasonable within itself, *and not opposed to some specific rule of law* [emphasis added].

In Texas a Federal court has recognized that students are entitled to the protection of the Fourth Amendment, at least off school property. The case involved a warrantless search of two high school boys and their car by the police.[13] Marijuana was found and the students were subsequently expelled from school, although the search had taken place off campus and did not involve school officials. A law suit was brought to reinstate the boys. The court held that the search of the students had been illegal, and therefore the marijuana could not be used as evidence against them in a school disciplinary proceeding any more than it could in a criminal prosecution.

A few school officials are aware of the danger of unlimited searching of students, which is somewhat encouraging. In its guide to student rights, the National Association of Secondary School Principals cautioned its members "against any such searching [of a student's person, desk, or locker] except under extreme circumstances, unless permission to do so has been freely given by the student, the student is present, and other competent witnesses are on hand."[14] An Ohio school administrator's guideline to student rights suggested that locker searches be made without a warrant or student consent only in cases of "imminent danger or harm."[15]

But these guidelines are only nice ideas until the courts recognize the students' constitutional protections in matters of in-school searches and seizures. Because you are so vulnerable legally in this area, it is particularly important that you protect yourself as fully as possible.

What can a student do to protect himself against searches of his person or property?

In case of the search of your person or locker, desk, etc., the best you can do is to follow these rules:

1) Your best protection is never to carry on you or keep in school anything that you wouldn't want the police or school officials to know about for any reason.

2) Never consent to any search. Say in a loud, clear voice, so that witnesses can hear, that you do not consent. *But do not resist* if a policeman or school official goes ahead with the search. If you don't consent to the search, there's a possibility that anything found on you will not be able to be used against you in court or in disciplinary proceedings. If you consent, it may be used.

Until the courts rule that the Fourth Amendment unambiguously applies to students in school, you should assume you may be searched.

NOTES

1. Formal Opinion of Counsel No. 67, 1 Ed. Dept. Rep. 766 (1952).
2. Delaware State Police Guide for School Administrators, approved Nov. 17, 1972.
3. *People v. Overton,* 20 N.Y. 2d 360 (1967), *vacated,* 393 U.S. 85 (1968), *reinstated on remand,* 24 N.Y. 2d 522 (1969).
4. *State v. Stein,* 203 Kan. 638, 456 P.2d. 1 (Kan. 1969), *cert. denied,* 397 U.S. 947 (1970).
5. *In re Donaldson,* 269 C.A. 2d 509, 75 Cal. Rptr. 220, (1969).

6. An excellent discussion of these cases in contained in a pamphlet by Professor William Buss, entitled "Legal Aspects of Crime Investigation in the Public Schools," published by National Organization of Legal Problems of Education, Topeka, Kansas.

7. *West Virginia State Board of Education v. Barnette*, 319 U.S. 624 (1943).

8. *Phillips v. Johns*, 12 Tenn. App. 354 (1930).

9. *People v. Jackson*, 319 N.Y.S. 2d 731, *aff'd*, 30 N.Y. 2d 734, (1970). But see, *People v. Bowers*, 339 N.Y.S. 2d 783 (N.Y.C. Crim. Ct., Kings Co., 1973).

10. *People v. Stewart*, 313 N.Y.S. 2d 253 (Crim. Ct. 1970); (1972); *Mercer v. State*, 450 S.W. 2d 715 (Tex. Civ. App. 1970).

11. *In re Gault*, 387 U.S.1 (1967).

12. *Hailey v. Brooks*, 191 S.W. 781, 783 (Tex. Civ. App. 1916).

13. *Caldwell v. Cannady*, Civil Actions No. 5-994, 5-1001, and 5-1002 (N.D. Tex. March 9, 1972).

14. Ackerly, *The Reasonable Exercise of Authority*, National Association of Secondary School Principals (1969).

15. *Rights and Responsibilities: Administrative Guidelines*, Division of Urban Education, Ohio Department of Education, Columbus, Ohio (1971).

VI

Corporal Punishment

Is it legal for public school officials to inflict corporal punishment on students?

The use of excessive physical force by school officials on students is illegal. The law regarding "moderate" physical force, or "corporal punishment," differs from state to state and in different school districts.

Some states, among them Massachusetts and New Jersey, have laws forbidding all corporal punishment in their public schools. Several other states have laws expressly permitting it. In Florida, for example, teachers may strike students but only after consultation with the principal. Montana permits corporal punishment only in the presence of another teacher or the principal and with notice to a parent or guardian, except in cases of open defiance, when no notice is required. Nevada only prohibits striking on the face or head.

Just because state law permits corporal punishment does not mean that a school must administer it. On the contrary, a number of school systems have passed their own regulations banning this form of punishment, among them Washington, D. C., New York City, Baltimore, Chicago, and in Pittsburgh from kindergarten through sev-

enth grade. The Oakland, California, school board, after a
suit was brought in Federal court, agreed to stop the use
of corporal punishment unless it was specifically requested
by a student's parents.[1]

It is significant that some of the largest school systems
in the country have banned corporal punishment, for an
argument often used in its favor is that it is impossible to
keep order and discipline in a school without the threat of
physical force. Clearly, if big schools in the midst of big
cities can function without the use of corporal punishment, so can smaller schools in small towns. The National
Education Association, a nation-wide organization of
teachers, has recommended the immediate abolition of
"infliction of physical pain upon students" for purposes of
discipline.[2]

What are the arguments against corporal punishment?

One argument is that corporal punishment has been
prohibited for many years in the military services and,
more recently, in prisons as well. In a case involving
physical force inflicted on prisoners in Arkansas, the court
held that the use of the strap "offends contemporary concepts of decency and human dignity and precepts of civi-
lization."[3]

A number of other arguments were made in a statement by Joyce Fiske of the Southern California Civil Liberties Union[4] before the Los Angeles Board of Education,
which subsequently voted to retain the practice.

Ms. Fiske pointed out that corporal punishment is ineffective and serves only to generate resentment in the
student: "Nobody has shown that it is in any way effective
in helping the student to develop more responsible, self-

disciplined behavior or even in helping other students and teachers be more secure. In fact, use of violence on such students generates rage, resentment, and hostility and may intensify the very behavior problems that triggered the punishment."

In answer to the argument that schools have insufficient resources to deal in any other way with behavioral problems than through physical force, she stated:

> The excuse of 'insufficient resources' has been used to justify cruel and harsh treatment now made illegal in most institutions, such as mental hospitals, prisons, army and navy. . . . But more importantly when we talk about insufficient resources, we must ask ourselves what justifies punishing [children] if a poorly functioning social system or an unfair and inadequate tax structure fails to provide for their needs?

* * *

A variation of the above argument about resources, is that we can't get rid of corporal punishment until we have provided alternatives, but so long as there is the institutionalizing of corporal punishment it will be a barrier to the development of other alternatives. Another defense of corporal punishment is that "this is the only language that some children understand." A system which allows teachers and principals to base their behavior on this perception is truly bankrupt. . . . If this is what some young people understand, it is up to the schools, which are supposed to be centers for learning and growth, to teach them a new language.

Some school officials have justified the status quo by saying parents and/or students want it. A well-known

psychologist has commented on this familiar form of
reasoning: "Children may ask for drugs and adults
too but that doesn't mean we give it to them. Besides,
while some young people through disruptive behavior
seem to 'ask for punishment' these may be the very
students most in need of help. [As for parents want-
ing corporal punshment,] schools often do not give in
to parents' demands, nor should they when those demands violate principles of sound education and mental health.

Sometimes school administrators argue that abolish-
ment of corporal punishment couldn't be achieved
without staff development and extensive retraining.
What a shocking comment—that complete re-educa-
tion of our educators would be necessary in order to
run the schools without hitting children. Even if it
were true, and for many dedicated, sensitive, and
humane teachers and principals it would not be true,
such an argument evades the central question that
must be asked: "Is this policy good for young people?" According to nearly unanimous expert testimony, according to the most modern insights and information drawn from a variety of professional dis-
ciplines, according to informed community opinion,
it is not."

Some or all of the arguments advanced by Joyce Fiske
have been made in several law suits challenging the use of
corporal punishment, but the results thus far have not
been encouraging. In New Mexico a federal court held
that "[s]chool officials have the power to promulgate and
enforce reasonable regulations governing students in attendance, with power to impose responsible nondiscrimi-
natory corporal punishment for breaches thereof, without

violating any federally protected constitutional rights of pupils.[5]

A Pennsylvania federal court agreed that the use of reasonable physical force does not constitute cruel and unusual punishment. It went on to say, however, that the decision concerning the use of corporal punishment should be made by the parent, not the state, and for that reason held that it could not be inflicted on a child whose parents notified the school that they did not wish it.[6]

Other suits challenging the use of physical punishment in schools are pending in Los Angeles[7] and Florida.[8]

When is corporal punishment "excessive," and what can a student do about it?

Both state and federal courts have held that a student can sue a teacher who injures him in the course of administering corporal punishment even though the use of physical force is legal in that state.

In an Illinois case, for example, the court held that while it had "no doubt of the right of a teacher to inflict corporal punishment in the process of enforcing discipline," the teacher might be guilty of battery if he acted "wantonly or maliciously."[9]

A federal court in Tennessee held that a teacher, accused of injuring a student by pulling a chair from under him, might be liable for damages if the student's injuries were proven to be serious or if the teacher's act was shown to have been motivated by racial prejudice.[10]

If you hope to prove excessive force, you must show both that it was unreasonable and unnecessary under the circumstances and that you actually suffered injury. The kind of evidence that might be presented to a court includes medical reports, photographs, and testimony of witnesses; therefore, it is important to see a doctor so you will have proof of your injuries.

NOTES

1. *Smith v. Jackson,* Civil Action No. C-70-1192-RFP. (N.D. Cal.)
2. Report of the Task Force on Corporal Punishment, National Education Association (1972).
3. *Jackson v. Bishop,* 404 F.2d 571 (8th Cir. 1968).
4. Quoted in "Corporal Punishment in the Public Schools" ACLU report (March, 1972).
5. *Sims v. Board of Education of Independent School District No. 22,* 329 F.Supp. 2d 678 (D.N.M. 1971); see also, *Ware v. Estes,* 328 F.Supp. 657, aff'd 458 F.2d 1360 (5th Cir. 1972), *cert den.* 41 U.S.L.W. 3288 (Nov. 13, 1972).
6. *Glaser v. Marietta,* 351 F.Supp. 555 (W.D.Pa. Nov. 1, 1972).
7. *Fiske v. Board of Education of the City of Los Angeles,* No. C22276 (Superior Court of California for L.A. County).
8. *Ingraham v. Wright,* Civ. No. 73-2078 (5th Cir.).
9. *City of Macomb v. Gould,* 244 N.E. 2d 634, 104 Ill. App. 2d 361 (1969).
10. *Patton v. Bennett,* 304 F.Supp. 297 (E.D. Tenn. 1969).

VII

Discrimination

It should go without saying that you have a right not to be discriminated against in school on the basis of race, religion, or ethnic background. Racial segregation within the public schools has been a major political and legal concern of the nation since 1954 when, in the case of *Brown* v. *Board of Education*,[1] the United States Supreme Court ruled that separate schools for different races were by definition not equal, and segregated public schools were therefore in violation of the equal protection clause of the Fourteenth Amendment. Hundreds of cases involving different aspects of school segregation—*de facto* segregation, racial imbalance, freedom of choice, busing, token integration, housing patterns—have gone to the courts since that landmark decision, and most decisions have clarified or extended the right of students to integrated schooling. The matter, unfortunately, is still not settled and will not be for many years to come.

If you feel that you are meeting discrimination in your school because of your race, ethnic background, or religion, you should take the matter to a community group that focuses on such problems or to a lawyer knowledgeable in segregation cases.

It is also illegal for public schools to discriminate against students on the basis of sex. Some school officials who have grown sensitive to racial and ethnic discrimination, however, still discriminate against females. (A later chapter will discuss the problem of pregnant girls and mothers, who are often subjected to different treatment than fathers.)

May girls be prohibited from taking "boys' " courses such as shop?

No. If you are prevented because of your sex from taking any course or from participating in any school activity that you are able to do, you have a good argument that you are the victim of unlawful discrimination. The same argument can be made if you are forced to take a course (such as sewing for girls or metal-working for boys) or to help with certain chores just because you're a female or you're a male.

In New York the state legislature has passed a law prohibiting sex discrimination in schools. It says: "No person shall be refused admission into or be excluded from any course of instruction offered in the State public and high school systems by reason of that person's sex." Massachusetts has a similar law.

In other places it has been necessary to bring law suits to end discrimination. A case brought in federal court in New York in which school officials agreed to admit girls into all-boys courses, such as shop and metal-working,[2] may have been instrumental in forcing the state legislature to pass its law against discrimination on the basis of sex.

Two similar law suits were settled out of court in California. In those cases school officials agreed to allow girls to take auto shop[3] and wood shop[4], courses that had previously been limited to boys.

Can a public school have fixed quotas of girls and boys?

One federal court has held that this practice constitutes discrimination on the basis of sex. A Boston school that required an entrance examination had fixed numbers of seats for boys and girls, as a result of which the boys' scores were measured against boys' and the girls' against girls'. Consequently some boys were admitted with lower scores than those achieved by some girls who were not admitted.

The court held that all applicants had to be measured against each other and those with the highest grades be admitted regardless of sex.[5]

Are all-male or all-female public schools permissible?

If a school offers a special program that may not be obtained in another school, it is illegal to exclude members of either sex from that school.[6] The fact that there are more jobs for male engineers than for women, for example, is not a legally acceptable reason for excluding women from a technical school or for taking a higher proportion of male applicants.

Can school officials prohibit girls from playing on school athletic teams?

At least one court has held that, where no alternative

competitive sports programs for girls were provided by the school, and where the girls in question—a tennis player, a cross-country runner, and a skier—could compete effectively on the boys teams, they could not be prohibited from doing so on the basis of sex.[7] The court recognized the fact that physiological differences between males and females would prevent most girls from competing on an equal level with the majority of boys. But this fact, the court stated, does not justify a rule against all females participating in sports with males without taking into consideration the capabilities of the individual girl.

The New York Commissioner of Education has promulgated rules permitting girls to participate in noncontact sports with boys; and as a result of an agreement reached in a New Jersey case,[8] girls in that state may try out for noncontact varsity teams if there is no separate interscholastic team for girls.

In Nebraska a federal court issued an injunction to prevent school officials from excluding a female student from the boys' golf team.[9] Noting that there was no girls' interschool team, the court observed: "Even though the defendants argue that she is free to play golf even though she is not a member of the school's team, the values she seeks cannot be lightly set aside. The state affords interschool competition and instruction at some expense and effort, surely for the reason that it and the defendants think that the program is of benefit to the participants. If the program is valuable for boys, is it of no value for girls?"

When girls were provided with an adequate athletic program of their own, a court in Illinois refused to order that they be permitted to participate in the boys' program.[10] The Michigan legislature, on the other hand, passed a law specifically permitting female students to participate in non-contact sports with males, even if the school also had an all-girls team.[11] This act was further supported by a Michigan federal court decision.[12]

Another way girls are often discriminated against in the area of physical education is that much more money is spent on boys' gym programs than girls'. A complaint against this practice is now pending before a New York federal court.[13]

NOTES

1. 347 U.S. 483 (1954).
2. *Sanchez v. Baron,* Civil Action No. 69 C 1615 (E.D.N.Y. March 22, 1973).
3. *Della Casa v. South San Francisco Unified School District,* Civ. Action No. 171-673 (San Mateo Sup. Ct.)
4. *Seward v. Clayton Valley High School District,* Civ. Action No. 134173 (Contra Costa Sup. Ct.).
5. *Bray v. Lee,* 337 F.Supp. 934 (D. Mass. 1972). But see, *Berkelman v. San Francisco Unified School District,* Civil No. C71 1875 LHB (N.D. Cal. Dec. 19, 1972).
6. *Kirstein v. Rector and Visitors of University of Virginia,* 309 F.Supp. 184 (E.D. Va. 1970).
7. *Brenden v. Independent School District #742,* 342 F.Supp. 1224 (D. Minn. 1972), *aff'd* 477 F.2d 1292 (8th Cir. 1973).
8. *Selden v. State Board of Education of New Jersey,* Civil Action No. 202-72 (D. N.J. 1972).
9. *Reed v. Nebraska School Activities Association,* 341 F.Supp. 258 (D. Neb. 1972).
10. *Bucha v. Illinois High School Association,* 351 F.Supp. 69 (N.D. Ill. E.D. 1972).
11. M.C.L.A. 340.379(2), Pub. Act. No. 138 (Mich. May 22, 1972).
12. *Morris v. Michigan State Board of Education,* Civ. Action No. 72-1578 (6th Cir. Jan. 25, 1973).
13. *Purdy v. Lane,* 73 Civ. 257 (N.D.N.Y.).

VIII

Tracking and Classification

What is tracking?

Tracking, or ability grouping, is the system of placing students in separate classes according to their supposed intelligence or aptitude.

In theory tracking may not seem to be such a bad idea, and in some schools it may be working well. But the practice—which exists in over 90% of American schools today—is coming under increasing attack from both courts and educators for the following reasons:

1. The placement of students in different ability groups is affected in large part by racial and socioeconomic factors; thus white, middle-class students end up in the college preparatory classes while poor and minority students end up in the slow and vocational-training classes. Sometimes this separation results from the race and class bias of those making the placements; sometimes from the use of standardized tests, which are culturally biased (that is, the questions draw on the experiences of middle-class rather than poor children). In the words of a judge who held the tracking system in Washington, D.C., to be unconstitutionally discriminatory:

Because these tests are standardized primarily on and are relevant to a white middle-class group of students, they produce inaccurate and misleading test scores when given to lower class and Negro students. As a result, rather than being classified according to ability to learn, these students are in reality being classified according to their socioeconomic or racial status, or—more precisely—according to environmental and psychological factors which have nothing to do with innate ability.[1]

2. Students are usually placed in tracks based on tests given in the first few grades of elementary school, thus prejudicing those "late bloomers" whose abilities develop when they are older. Since students in many schools are never tested again, they end up being confined to a track that does not reflect their true abilities or potential.

3. Many schools have a grading system that prohibits teachers of students in lower tracks from giving higher than a certain maximum grade, such as 80, no matter how well a student performs, and at the same time prohibits teachers of students in higher tracks from giving grades lower than 80. The effect is to prevent mobility between tracks.

4. The academic achievement of a student placed in a lower track frequently declines the longer he stays in school. Placed in a slow track, he, his teacher, and everyone else comes to think of him as slow and incapable of academic success. He is defined as "a dumb person." No one expects much from him, and he doesn't expect much from himself.

One noted educator described the process in these words:

These children, by and large, do not learn because they are not being taught effectively, and they are not being taught because those who are charged with the responsibility of teaching them do not believe that they can learn, do not expect that they can learn, and do not act toward them in ways which help them to learn.[2]

The stigma that students often feel upon being assigned to a low track—and the resulting sense of despair and hopelessness—was poignantly expressed by one student, who said:

It really don't have to be the tests, but after the tests, there shouldn't be no separation in the classes. Because, as I say again, I felt good when I was with my class, but when they went and separated us— that changed us. That changed our ideas, our thinking, the way we thought about each other and turned us to enemies toward each other—because they said I was dumb and they were smart.

When you first go to junior high school you do feel something inside—it's like ego. You have been from elementary to junior high, you feel great inside. You say, well daggone, I'm going to deal with the *people* here now, I am in junior high school. You get this shirt that says Brown Junior High or whatever the name is and you are proud of that shirt. But then you go up there and the teacher says—"Well, so and so, you're in the basic section, you can't go with the other kids." The devil with the whole thing—you lose —something in you—like it just goes out of you.[3]

5. Despite the promise of special, compensatory instruction for students in lower tracks, in fact they often receive

an education substantially inferior to that received by students in the higher tracks. Sometimes, for example, the lower tracks are given more gym or shop and fewer hours of classroom instruction. In some schools, they use facilities, equipment and books that are inferior to those used in the higher tracks. Not surprisingly teachers are often less interested in students they expect to be dull. Frequently it is the less competent teachers who are assigned to teach the lower tracks.

6. Placement in a low track in school can condemn a student to a "low track" for the rest of his life, for his job possibilities upon graduation are severely limited by the kind of education he has received. As the system worked in Washington, D.C.:

> Those in the lower tracks [were], for the most part, molded for various levels of vocational assignments; those in the upper tracks, on the other hand, [were] given the opportunity to prepare for the higher ranking jobs and most significantly, for college. . . .[4]

7. In schools where a tracking system is particularly rigid and separation between the tracks is nearly complete, students frequently become polarized along racial or class lines. The result is tension and hostility that not only undermine the educational atmosphere, but also strengthen barriers out of school between races or classes —barriers that our society is supposedly committed to eliminating. Moreover the consequence of separating black from white and rich from poor is that students are deprived of the educational and cultural enrichment that comes from sharing experiences with those of different backgrounds.

Can a student challenge placement in a low track?

No court cases bear directly on this point, but there are indications that courts would uphold a student's demand for a hearing to determine whether he was in the right track and for periodic reevaluation of the placement. This has been done in cases involving the placement of students in schools for disturbed and retarded children.[5]

In challenging tracking, you should find out the criteria used for making placements in a given track. For example, in a New York school it was discovered that one factor was the desire of school officials to have an equal number of boys and girls in each class; thus some students were placed in tracks lower than those for which their test scores qualified them.

Your chances of changing your placement are particularly strong if the track you were put in is a vocational one that provides an entirely different type of education from the highest track (rather than the same courses on a less advanced level). If you want to be in a college preparatory course, that decision should be yours and not the guidance counsellor's. You should not let anyone cut off the possibility of your going to college by putting you in a general or vocational track against your will just because your grades are low or no one else in your family ever went to college, or for any other reason. You should demand whatever type of education you want.

Can a student challenge his placement in a special school for disturbed or retarded children or his exclusion from regular school?

Yes. There have been several recent court cases involving the exclusion of children from school for medical or behavior reasons and their placement in special schools without adequate review.

A Pennsylvania court ordered that a number of due-process procedures must be followed "whenever any mentally retarded or allegedly mentally retarded child, aged five years, six months, through twenty-one years, is recommended for a change in educational status by a school district, intermediate unit or any school official."[6]

The procedures ordered by this court included detailed notice of the reasons for the proposed action, such as test scores and reports. It called for parents to be notified of their "right to contest the proposed action at a full hearing . . . in a place and at a time convenient to the parent, before the proposed action may be taken; . . . to be represented at the hearing by legal counsel, to examine before the hearing his child's school records including any tests or reports upon which the proposed action may be based, to present evidence of [their] own, including expert medical, psychological, and educational testimony, and to confront and to cross-examine any school official . . . who may have evidence upon which the proposed action may be based."

The court specified that the hearing is to be public unless the parents want it closed, a transcript is to be made, and the decision of the hearing officer is to be based only on the evidence presented at the hearing. Further, the burden of proof is on the school to justify the move (rather than making the student prove that he shouldn't be moved). The court also ordered the reevaluation every two years of the placement of students in special schools.

In California a federal court issued an order prohibiting the use of standardized I.Q. test results as the basis for placement in "Educable Mentally Retarded" classes. The court noted that even the school officials who had been sued apparently conceded that the tests were culturally biased, and that some school districts (New York City perhaps being the most prominent) have stopped using I.Q. tests altogether.[7]

Another lawsuit attacked the practice whereby some students, whose primary language was not English, were mistakenly placed in classes for the mentally handicapped. As a result of an agreement filed in court, all such students will have their placements re-evaluated and, in the future, appropriate testing and examination will be administered to insure that language and cultural factors will determine school placement.[8]

The basis of these decisions is the courts' recognition that placement in a special class or school may have a serious impact on a child's life and, if he disagrees with that placement, he should have an opportunity to be heard.

NOTES

1. *Hobson v. Hansen*, 269 F.Supp. 401 (D. D.C. 1967).
2. Clark, *Dark Ghetto* (1965).
3. *Schafer, et al*, "Programmed for Social Class: Tracking in High School," *Transaction* (Oct. 1970).
4. *Hobson v. Hansen*, 269 F.Supp. 401 (D. D.C. 1967).

5. *Mills v. Board of Education of the District of Columbia,* 348 F.Supp. 866 (D. D.C. 1972); *Pennsylvania Association for Retarded Children v. Commonwealth of Pennsylvania,* 334 F.Supp. 1257 (E.D. Pa. 1971).
6. *Pennsylvania Association for Retarded Children v. Commonwealth of Pennsylvania,* 334 F.Supp. 1257 (E.D. Pa. 1971); see also, *Mills v. Board of Education of the District of Columbia,* 348 F.Supp. 866 (D. D.C. 1972).
7. *Larry P. v. Riles,* 343 F.Supp. 1306 (N.D. Cal. 1972).
8. *Guadalupe Organization, Inc. v. Tempe Elementary School District,* Civ. No. 71-435 PHX (D. Ariz., Jan. 24, 1972).

IX

Marriage, Pregnancy, Parenthood

It is common practice for schools to prohibit students from attending school or participating in extracurricular activities when they get married or become pregnant or have children. These rules frequently curtail the education of such students at a time when it is most crucial for many of them to continue going to school.

School administrators advance a variety of reasons for their policies penalizing married and pregnant students, but in most cases the true reason turns out to be a moral one: the officials don't want students knowing or thinking or talking about sex. If a young married man is permitted to continue to play on the high school football team, they say, he may tell his teammates in the locker room about his sexual relations with his wife. If students see a pregnant classmate in school, particularly if she is unmarried, some school officials fear they may become morally contaminated; and as one school official so delicately put it, he wouldn't want students to think the school condoned

111

"conduct on the part of unmarried students of a nature
to cause pregnancy."[1]

Clearly these ideas are considerably outdated. The aver-
age high school student today is constantly exposed to
books, movies, and magazines full of explicit sexual material, which makes it rather unlikely that a locker room conversation or the sight of a pregnant girl would have any
effect at all. It is impossible for schools to protect students from sexual knowledge, whether vicarious or first-
hand. Courts are beginning to recognize this fact.

Do students have a right to continue going to school if they get married?

As early as 1929, a court in Mississippi held that a high
school could not expel a student for getting married.[2]

Thirty-five years later a Kentucky Court, held that there
was "no reason to suppose that the marriage of a student
would diminish the need of that student for an education
—indeed, just the contrary would appear the case."[3] In
Texas a state court ordered a married couple[4] and a married girl[5] reinstated in school upon finding that none of
them had been found guilty of "incorrigible" or improper
conduct by getting married.

Do pregnant girls have a right to attend school?

Not surprisingly, the cases have been more favorable to
pregnant girls who are married than to those who are unmarried. But in either case, if a school expels a student
against her wishes because she is pregnant, she has a

sound legal argument that she is being discriminated against and arbitrarily deprived of her legal right to an education.

Although there are cases upholding a school's right to expel pregnant students, especially unmarried ones, the trend is in the opposite direction. In Massachusetts a federal court ordered school officials to restore an unmarried pregnant girl to the status of a regular student.[6] The court found that school officials had not met their burden of proving a "likelihood that her presence would cause any disruption of or interference with school activities or pose a threat of harm to others." The court was not persuaded by the school principal's argument that, by her continued presence, the school board would appear to be condoning premarital relations. Where such arguments of morality, as opposed to the pregnant girl's health, are advanced as the basis for suspension, girls may argue that they are being irrationally discriminated against if the young men responsible for their pregnancies are not also removed from school.[7]

A number of school boards are beginning to take a more enlightened attitude regarding pregnancy Among the best policies is one adopted in New York City in 1968 which allows students the option of remaining in their regular schools throughout their entire pregnancy or of attending a full school program at a special center.[8] New York City school principals have even been provided with emergency instructions on what to do if a student goes into labor.

The Philadelphia Board of Education has established a policy that pregnant students may continue in their regular schools until the sixth month of pregnancy and may return to their regular schools as soon as medically able at the end of pregnancy. The regulation adds that the students should be retained on the school roll and provided assignments while at home during the last trimester of pregnancy.[9] The Maryland State Board of Education likewise ordered that pregnant girls, either married or unmarried, may remain in the full, regular school program throughout their pregnancies and that any decision to change a pregnant student's school program must be made in consultation with medical personnel and the girl herself.[10]

Can students who have children attend school?

Students who are parents, married or unmarried, have a number of court cases backing up their right to stay in school.

A court in Kansas in 1929 ruled that a married student with a child had a right to attend high school if she wished. The court stated:

> The public schools are for the benefit of children within school age, and efficiency ought to be the sole object of those charged with the power and privilege of managing and conducting the same; and while great care should be taken to preserve order and proper discipline, it is proper also to see that no one within school age should be denied the privilege of attending school unless it is clear that the public interest demands the expulsion of such pupils or a denial of his right to attend.[11]

Forty years later, a federal court reached the same conclusion and ordered Mississippi school officials to readmit two unmarried mothers to high school unless the officials could show on a fair hearing that the young women were "so lacking in moral character that their presence in the schools [would] taint the education of other students."[12] The court held that the mere fact that a girl had borne a child out of wedlock "does not forever brand her as a scarlet woman undeserving of any chance for rehabilitation or the opportunity for future education." The court came to this conclusion even though it believed that an unmarried mother had committed "a wrong." No mention was made of unwed fathers.[13]

A Texas court ordered the admission of a young mother to high school simply on the grounds that she was entitled to an education under a state law furnishing school funds for people of her age.[14]

Do married students and students with children have the right to participate in extracurricular activities?

School officials frequently argue that while attending school may be a right, participating in extracurricular activities is a privilege from which students can be arbitrarily barred. This argument would seem to have little merit in view of the court decisions finding extracurricular activities to be an essential aspect of education and of the well-established legal principle that even privileges cannot be denied by the state arbitrarily.

Almost without exception, recent court decisions have declared illegal rules that penalize students who are married or have children.

A Federal court in Tennessee held that the rule excluding a married girl student from all school activities except classes infringed on her fundamental right to marry by severely limiting her right to an education. Since marriage was legal and consonant with the public policy of Tennessee, the court said, school officials could not punish a student for her married status.[15] This was also the reasoning of a court in Ohio.[16]

An Indiana court refused to accept several justifications presented by school officials for their policy of excluding married students from interscholastic sports.[17] To the argument that married students should spend their time discharging family economic responsibilities instead of playing sports, the court replied that this reason might or might not be justified for both married and unmarried students. Furthermore, the court said, a married man is presumed to be mature enough to make the proper decisions concerning his family responsibilities by himself. As for sex talk in the locker room, the court pointed out that if such talk were going to take place, there were many other opportunities, since married students were not segregated at any other point during the school day.

The same result was reached by a Montana federal court, which held that school officials could not prohibit a married student from playing on the high school football team, thereby depriving him of the chance to win a college scholarship. The court found that the school officials had not presented sufficient evidence to show that married students' participation in extracurricular activities would result in a reasonable likelihood of "moral pollution, disruption or disciplinary problems" within the student body.[18]

Recognizing that a student's record of participation in extracurricular activities often influenced his ability to get into college, a Texas court ordered school officials to permit a divorced student who had put her child up for adoption to participate in extracurricular activities.[19] A

New Jersey federal court has also enjoined school officials from discriminating against students with respect to participation in extra-curricular activities solely on the basis of their marital or parental status.[20] The Idaho Attorney General has issued an opinion declaring that marriage alone is not a reason for barring students from extra-curricular activities.[21]

Do pregnant students have the right to attend graduation?

In New York the State Commissioner of Education overrode the decision of a local board of education to prohibit a married pregnant student from attending her high school graduation. He held that decision to be "clearly arbitrary, capricious and unreasonable" since the young woman had met all of the academic requirements.[22]

The point to stress in any dispute with school officials involving pregnancy or marital or parental status is that the burden is on them to show the rational relationship between the regulation and the functioning of the school. If no such relationship can be shown, as is usually the case, the exclusion violates your right under the Fourteenth Amendment not to be arbitrarily and capriciously deprived of an education.

Do married students, pregnant students and students with children have a right *not* to attend school?

Yes. Most school systems will allow students who are married, pregnant, or have children to drop out of school, even though they are under the compulsory school age.

Where schools have refused to grant such permission, courts have decided in favor of letting the students leave school.[23]

NOTES

1. *Ordway v. Hargraves*, 323 F.Supp. 1155 (D. Mass. 1971).
2. *McLeod v. Mississippi*, 154 Miss. 468, 122 So. 737 (1929).
3. *Kentucky Board of Education v. Bentley*, 383 S.W. 2d 677 (1964).
4. *Carrollton-Farmers Branch Independent School District, v. Knight*, 418 S.W.2d 535 (Tex. Ct. of Civ. App. 1967).
5. *Anderson v. Canyon Independent School District*, 412 S.W.2d 387 (Tex. Ct. Civ. App. 1967).
6. *Ordway v. Hargraves*, 323 F.Supp. 1155 (D.C. Mass. 1971).
7. *Farley v. Reinhart*, Civil Action No. 15569 (N.D. Ga. Sept. 29, 1971).
8. *Education of Pregnant Students*, Special Circular No. 10, Board of Education of the City of New York (1968–69).
9. *Policy in Regard to Educational Programs. Withdrawals and Readmission of Pregnant Girls*, File #440, School District of Philadelphia (1968).
10. Resolution No. 1967–43, Maryland State Board of Education (July 26, 1967).
11. *Nutt v. Board of Education*, 128 Kan. 507, 278 Pa. 1065 (1929).
12. *Perry v. Grenada Municipal Separate School District*, 300 F.Supp. 748 (N.D. Miss. 1969).
13. The same court subsequently applied its decision in *Perry* to another school district: *Shull v. Columbus Municipal Separate School District*, 338 F.Supp. 1376 (N.D. Miss 1972).
14. *Alvin Independent School District v. Cooper*, 404 S.W. 2d 76 (Tex. Ct. of Civ. App. 1966).
15. *Holt v. Shelton*, 341 F.Supp. 821 (M.D. Tenn. 1972).
16. *Davis v. Meek*, 344 F.Supp. 298, (N.D. Ohio 1972).
17. *Wellsand v. Valparaiso Community Schools Corporation*, Civil Action No. 71 H122 (2) (N.D. Ind. 1971).

18. *Moran* v. *School District #7, Yellowstone County,* 350 F.Supp. 1180 (D. Mont. 1972) See also, *Hollon* v. *Mathis Independent School District,* 358 F.Supp. 1269 (S.D. Tex. 1973).
19. *Romans* v. *Crenshaw,* 354 F.Supp. 868 (S.D. Tex. 1972).
20. *Johnson* v. *Board of Educ.,* Civ. Action No. 172-70, (D.N.J. April 17, 1970).
21. Idaho Attorney General Opinion, November 3, 1969.
22. *Matter of Murphy,* 11 Ed. Dept. Rep. 180 (New York Commissioner of Education, 1972).
23. *State* v. *Priest,* 210 La. 389, 27 So. 2d 173 (1946); *In re Goodwin,* 214 La. 1062, 39 So. 2d 731 (1949); *In re Rogers,* 234 N.Y.S. 2d 172 (1962).

X

School Records

Every school makes a record of each student's academic and personal progress from the time he enters kindergarten until he graduates, and often it keeps this "cumulative record" for many years afterward. The record may include, as was noted in one New York case, "progress reports, subject grades, intelligence quotients, tests, achievement scores, medical records, psychological and psychiatric reports, selective guidance notes and the evaluations of students by educators."[1] In short, your school keeps a great deal of personal information about you permanently on file. As the official school handbook given to all entering students in one New York City high school says, "Long after you have graduated, inquiries concerning your record are answered by consulting your record card. This is truly a permanent one. Make it a good one."

The National Education Association's *Code of Student Rights and Responsibilities* states: "Records are kept to assist the school in offering appropriate educational experiences to the student. The interest of the student must supersede all other purposes to which records might be put."

In fact, the reverse is often the case. School officials

frequently use a student's record against him as a threat ("If you do that again, it will go in your record and end up in your college recommendations.") or as the basis for a suspension or other serious disciplinary action. Often the information contained in school records is little more than an expression of personal opinion of the student by teachers and other school personnel. Such remarks as "[student] spoke strangely to girls in class"; "never gives anyone benefit of doubt"; "Black militant"; and "disrespectful while class was saluting flag" have appeared in the permanent records of students in the New York City schools.

At least one court has recognized that student records are not supposed to be gossip sheets, and it ordered a high school principal to expunge from a student's record a notation that he had criticized the school and the principal on a radio program.[2] New Hampshire specifically bars schools from keeping records "which reflect the political activities or beliefs of students." It is also one of the few states that require that cumulative records be destroyed when they are no longer current.

The biggest problems that arise in connection with school records involve the matter of who has access to them. On the one hand, many schools maintain that records are so confidential that the student and his parents cannot see them; on the other, schools frequently allow anyone else who claims to have a legitimate interest— such as a policeman, social worker, potential employer on draft board—to see these same confidential records. The right to have petty personal comments expunged from your record doesn't mean much if you cannot find out they are there; and even without gossip, your record contains personal information that you probably would not want many people to see. Fortunately the law is beginning to

develop so as to expand the student's right of access to his
own record while limiting the public's right to see it.

**Do students and their parents have a right to see the
student's own school records?**

If you or your parents are denied access to your school
records, you should first check your state's education law
and school board regulations. In many places the right to
see your records is granted by one or the other. For example: in Oregon parents have the right under state law
to inspect all of their children's school records,[3] in Maine[4]
and Idaho[5] both students and parents can see the records,
and in New Mexico any student in a public school is
guaranteed the right to inspect his school record.[6] Most
other states have broad statutes that give citizens access to
all public records that, presumably, would support the right
of parents to see their children's school records. A number
of school districts—New York City, Des Moines, Iowa,
and Jefferson City, Missouri, are three such—have adopted
regulations permitting a student and/or his parent access
to a student's records.

Legal decisions have held that students or their parents
have a right to see the student's records. In New York,
the State Commissioner of Education established a basic
rule that a parent has the right to see his child's full school
record.[7] The Commissioner has emphasized that school officials are not free to deny parents the right to see certain records by calling them "confidential." *Any* records
that the school keeps on a student must be made available to the parents. As the commissioner said, "It is readily
apparent that no one has a greater right to such information than the parent. . . ."[8]

A similar view was expressed by a New York court, which upheld a father's right to see his son's school record: "It needs no further citation of authority to recognize the obvious 'interest' which a parent has in the school records of his child. We are, therefore, constrained to hold as a matter of law that the parent is entitled to inspect the records."[9] When a school official denied a student a copy of her grades and a transcript of her high school record on the grounds that the file was his personal property, another court held that records kept by teachers were not the property of the school and could not be withheld from the student.[10]

What can be done about improper or inaccurate entries in a student's record?

The best protection against the accumulation of irrelevant or inaccurate information in a student's file is for parents to regularly inspect their children's records. Part of the reason that school officials are able to keep records that are frequently based on little more than hearsay and rumor is their assumption that no parent or student will ever ask to see the records. If more parents demanded to see their students' records, school officials might be more careful in checking their facts.

New York City and the state of Washington have a safeguard plan that you might suggest your school adopt: students are permitted to contest the accuracy of any entry in their records and, if still not satisfied, to add their own version of the incident. In New York, parents also must be notified of any derogatory remark in their child's record and have the right to appeal to have it expunged.[11] These are protections that many teachers have won for themselves, and they may be willing to support such a policy for students. (Ask them.) The report of a conference of educators who studied school record policies suggested, as a means of protection, that schools create a panel to which students and parents could present challenges to records they considered inaccurate; if necessary, hearings would be held on particular challenges.[12]

Does a student have the right to have his school records kept confidential from outsiders?

Some states have statutes that prohibit schools from releasing information about students to the general public.[13] These laws do not go far enough, however, for while they may prohibit the release of your file to your next door neighbor, they often have exceptions permitting the release of the information to governmental agencies, such as government officers and social-service agencies.[14] A better statute is Oregon's, which has no such exceptions; it even specifically protects school staff members from being compelled to testify in a lawsuit about personal conversations with students where disclosure "would tend to damage or incriminate the student or his family."[15] The policy of the New Mexico State Board of Education explicitly notes "that government investigative agencies as such have no inherent legal right to have access to student files and records, and prohibits the release of information"[16] to government agencies without specific authorization from the student or a court order. Delaware and New York have similar rules. Finally a Mighican statute prohibits any school staff member from testifying in any court proceeding, civil or criminal, on the content of a student's record.[17]

In those states that do have full or partial confidentiality regulations regarding student records, a suit for damages would be possible if information about a student is released in violation of the policy.[18] Even without a statute a suit for damages might be successful against school personnel who divulge confidential communications of a student. At least one court has held that the special relationship between students and school officials places a duty of confidentiality on those officials.[19]

Few states or school districts have policies guaranteeing that a student's records or communications will be confidential. In fact, few school districts have any policy at all about who can see student records, even though information from them is frequently requested. The ACLU was informed that in one week, in the New York City schools, 28 different outside agencies requested, and received, information about students from school records. The agencies included the F.B.I., military intelligence, the police department, the Selective Service System, district attorneys, fraternal organizations, and labor unions. Even if well-meaning in their reasons for collecting information, these agencies have no business seeing your school records unless you and your parents want them to. If a social worker or a lawyer or a policeman wants to see what is in your record, or some section of your record, you or your parents should be the only ones to grant or deny permission. If you discuss with a guidance counselor a personal problem, such as drug use, you should have some assurance that records of that conversation will remain confidential. Unfortunately school officials and their employees rarely give—and sometimes are unable to give—such assurances.

The Des Moines, Iowa, and New York City school districts, and the state of Delaware require that a parent or student sign a release before information from the

student's records can be given out.[20] Written authorization
is required in New Mexico as a result of a policy adopted
by the State Board of Education in 1972; moreover, when
information from a student's record is subpoenaed or required under a court order, the student must be notified.

Some schools ask parents at the beginning of a school
year, or at the time when their children first enter, to sign
a form which, among other things, gives to the school the
authority to release at its own discretion information from
student records to inquiring outsiders. This kind of blanket
authorization leads to many abuses. A parent may be
happy to release certain information to a social worker
but unwilling to release the same information to the police
department. He may also change his mind about the release of his child's school record when certain new information is added. By requesting the parent to sign a blanket
authorization for release of information, the school is asking him to sign away a parent's discretionary rights concerning his own child. Instead, parents should ask that
their permission be obtained each time the school wishes
to release information.

If you want to fight your school's policy of releasing
information to outsiders, you can make the analogy both
to hospital records and youthful-offender records. Neither
of these can be released to the public or any government agency without the specific permission of the patient
or offender.

**At what age may students rather than their parents have
access to and control over the release of their school
records?**

The law varies from state to state and school district

to school district. Delaware, for example, permits students from the age of 14 to control the release of their own school records.[21] There are no court decisions on the subject.

Do students have the right to see college and job recommendations written for them by school officials?

One court in Maine has held that a college had to release to a rejected applicant the record it had been sent by his high school in order for the file to be used as evidence in a law suit against the high school officials.[22] The student claimed that the recommendation was unfair and untrue.

NOTES

1. *Matter of Thibadeau,* 1 Ed. Dept. Rep. 607 (New York Commissioner of Education 1960).
2. *Shakin v. Schuker,* Index No. 6312/71 (S. Ct. Queens Co. Nov. 16, 1971).
3. Oregon Rev. Stat. 336. 195 (1971).
4. Maine Rev. Stat. Ann., Title 1, Ch. 13, Sec. 405.
5. Recommended guidelines for Student Rights and Responsibilities of the Idaho State Board and Department of Education (1973).
6. Reg. #72-6 of the New Mexico State Board of Education, "Confidentiality of Student Records," effective February 25, 1972.
7. *Matter of Thibadeau,* 1 Ed. Dept. Rep. 607 (1960);
8. *Matter of Wilson,* 11 Ed. Dept. Rep. 208 (1972).
9. *Van Allen v. McCleary,* 211 N.Y.S. 2d 501 (S. Ct. 1961).
10. *Valentine v. Independent School District,* 174 N.W. 334 (Iowa 1919).

11. Special Circular No. 103 (1972-73) of the Board of Education of the City of New York.
12. "Guidelines for the Collection, Maintenance and Dissemination of Pupil Records: Report of a Conference on the Ethical and Legal Aspects of School Record Keeping," Russell Sage Foundation (1970).
13. See, e.g., Miss. Code Ann. (Supp. 1971) § 6225–01; N.H. Rev. Stat. Ann., Title VI, 91–A:5, §IV.
14. See e.g., West's Ann. Calif. Codes, Art. 6, §10751; N.J.S.A., Sec. 18A: 36–19.
15. Oregon Rev. Stat., 344.040 and §336.195 (1971).
16. Reg #72–6 of the New Mexico State Board of Education, "Confidentiality of Student Records," effective February 25, 1972.
17. Michigan Compiled Laws, §600.2165 (1968).
18. *Elder v. Anderson*, 23 Cal. Rptr. 48 (1962).
19. *Blair* v. *Union Free School Dist. #6, Hauppage,* 234 N.Y.S. 2d 222 (Dist. Ct., Suffolk Co. 1971).
20. *Release of School Information,* Des Moines Public Schools; Special Circular No. 103 (1972-73) of the Board of Education of the City of New York.
21. Title 14, Delaware Code, §4114 (1970.)
22. *Creel v. Brennan, et al,* Civil Action 3572, Sup. Ct. (Androscoggin County, Me. 1968).

XI

Grades and Diplomas

Can a student be denied a diploma for misconduct if he has fulfilled all academic requirements for graduation?

Although few legal precedents in this area have been established for public school students, a recent decision of the Chancellor of the New York City schools, binding on all high schools in that city, is significant. The ruling came out of the following situation. The New York high school diploma has always included some mention of "citizenship" as well as academic achievement. One principal, therefore, withheld temporarily the diploma of a student who, he felt, was not a "good citizen," even though the student had completed all his academic work for graduation. The student, who had been active both as a student government officer and as a leader of the black student organization, had put the school officials under pressure in his attempts to change school policies. When graduation time came, the student was informed that although he had won a college scholarship, his high school diploma would be withheld for six months because of some arguments he had had with school officials; he had not met the "citizenship" requirements for graduation. A district assistant superintendent upheld the principal's decision, but the Chancellor

overturned the original ruling and issued the diploma. He
stated:

> Students who violate rules of conduct are subject to
> disciplinary measures, but the manipulation of a di-
> ploma is not a proper or legitimate disciplinary tool
> in view of the inherent difficulty in defining "citizen-
> ship" and the clear danger and impropriety of label-
> ling students as "good" or "bad" citizens. The school
> system should award the diploma on the basis of
> carefully defined educational criteria, and not deny
> or delay the diploma on other than educational
> grounds or as a means of discipline. In brief, the
> school is empowered to grant diplomas, not citizen-
> ship.[1]

**Can school officials discipline a student by barring him
from graduation exercises?**

Again, the answer is probably not. In a 1971 case in
New York State, the court ruled that a school district
could not bar a high school student who had satisfactorily
completed her studies but who had allegedly struck and
threatened her principal during a disturbance at the school.
The court ruled there was no evidence that her presence
at graduation ceremonies would be disruptive, so that barring her from participating would not be "a reasonable
punishment meant to encourage the best educational results." It added: "It would indeed be a distortion of our
educational process in this period of youthful discontent-
ment to snatch from a young woman at the point of educational fruition the savoring of her educational success."[2]
Similarly the decision of a New York City junior high

school to bar a student from graduation exercises was reversed by the New York State Commissioner of Education because the grounds for her punishment—"lack of good citizenship"—were too vague. In addition, the Commissioner said, "It is educationally unsound for a school system to brand an individual with the label of 'poor citizen.' The placing of such a label upon a student is not a proper function of a school system."[3]

When a married and pregnant student was barred from graduation exercises because of her condition, the New York commissioner again overruled the school district's decision.[4]

Can a student's grade be lowered as a punishment for misbehavior or other nonacademic reasons?

Obviously if a diploma cannot be withheld for nonacademic reasons, it follows that grades cannot properly be lowered for similar reasons. Courts, however, generally will not review whether a student deserved a particular grade unless he can prove that it was given for a nonacademic reason.

If you simply disagree with your teacher about the quality of your work—you get a C and think you deserve an A—there isn't a court in the country that would substitute its judgment for the teacher's and give you the higher grade. If, on the other hand, you can prove that the teacher was acting arbitrarily or maliciously by giving you a low grade for reasons unrelated to the quality of your work, you have a chance of winning in court.

For example, a Vermont court agreed to hear a case involving the dismissal of a student from medical school for failure in a course[5] because the student claimed that his instructor had stated he would not give him a passing grade regardless of the quality of his work. The court said that under normal circumstances, it would not substitute its judgment for a teacher's on what a student's grade should be; but in this case the teacher's statement, if true, would have been arbitrary, capricious, and in bad faith. The court therefore held that the student should be given the chance to prove that he was failed for non-academic reasons.

Similarly a Florida court held that a state college student could not be expelled for failure to maintain academic standards when his offense had been one of bad conduct—getting out of a required course by improper means.[6]

Some high schools have recognized that grades should measure academic and not social performance. The guide to grading standards in one New York high school sets forth a good policy:

> Grades are estimates of academic achievement only. Pupils' behavior and attitude do not, in themselves, provide a legitimate basis for calculating grades. Evidences of excellence of deficiencies in character are to be recorded in other ways. . . . Continued absence or lateness should have an effect on the final grade only insofar as it affects actual achievement in the subject.

Can a student be denied a diploma for failing gym?

The law is unclear in most states. In New York, the State Commissioner of Education has ruled that a local board of education may not refuse graduation or promotion because of failure in physical education. Students, therefore, must be granted diplomas even if they are not able to perform certain required physical exercises.[7]

The Commissioner has not ruled on the denial of a diploma when a student regularly cuts his gym class, but he has held that a local board may not ignore the refusal of a student to participate in physical education throughout the school year and deny him graduation or advancement without warning.[8] Some advance notice stating the maximum number of permissible absences and a warning of the possibility of not graduating is required.

With the law as unclear as it is, students run a clear risk in not attending gym class. If an attempt is made to keep you from graduating because you cut gym, you should determine if you were given any advance notice of such a possibility. In addition, you might try to show that other students are exempt from gym, such as honor guard members and night students. If school officials claim that physical exercise is necessary to earn a diploma, it is fair to ask why that requirement is made of you and not them.

NOTES

1. *Matter of Carroll*, Decision of Chancellor (December 6, 1971). See also, *Matter of Wilson*, 11 Ed. Dept. Rep. 208 (New York State Commissioner of Education 1972).
2. *Ladson v. Board of Education, Union Free School District #9*, 323 N.Y.S. 2d 545 (S. Ct. 1971).
3. *Matter of Wilson*, 11 Ed. Dept. Rep. 208 (1972).
4. *Matter of Murphy*, 11 Ed. Dept. Rep. 180 (1972).
5. *Connelly v. University of Vermont and State Agricultural College*, 244 F.Supp. 156 (D. Vt. 1965).

6. *Woody v. Burns*, 188 So. 2d 56 (Dist. Ct. App. Fla. 1966).
7. *Matter of Cohen*, 1 Ed. Dept. Rep. 689 (1961).
8. *Matter of Rafferty*, 11 Ed. Dept. Rep. 53 (1971).

Afterword

The preceding chapters have tried to describe what legal rights students have in a public school. At this point, or even earlier, it may occur to you that students at your school in fact have few of these rights. Can you do anything about it? As we mentioned at the outset, there are not enough lawyers available to bring lawsuits to secure every right of every student. So just as a practical matter, you may well have to consider other means for securing them. Sometimes, in fact, it is preferable to use other means, whether or not lawyers are available. Lawsuits can take months to resolve and, of course, may finally be lost, leaving the school policy unchanged. Many students, moreover, believe that broader and more permanent change in school policy results when students are involved in bringing about change than when a court declares a specific practice illegal.

There is, finally, perhaps a more important reason why lawyers should not be relied on too extensively. Although lawyers can be helpful in dealing with the range of problems discussed in this book, students remain unfree in a variety of other ways, big and small, which are part of the accepted routine at most schools and which no lawyer will be able to challenge through the courts.

Underlying this unfree condition is "the assumption that the state has the right to compel adolescents to spend six or seven hours a day, five days a week, 36 or so weeks a year, in a specific place, under the charge of a particular group of persons in whose selection they have no voice, performing tasks about which they have no choice, without remuneration and subject to specialized regulations and sanctions that are applicable to no one else in the community nor to them except in this place."[1] That is an assumption that no court has yet directly challenged. Indirectly, yes, by declaring that students do have some rights. But for even those rights to be most meaningful, they must be directed towards establishing the proposition that students "have the right to influence the effects the institution has on them. As other institutions exist to serve their clients, schools at all levels exist so that people attending them can learn. More than most institutions, schools influence the course of their clients' present and future lives. Students therefore have the right to substantial influence over the educational program, including the goals they pursue, the topics they study, the learning materials and learning processes they use, and the criteria for evaluating accomplishment."[2]

A variety of means are available to students to secure a greater degree of participation in running their schools. It is beyond the scope of this book to suggest the most effective means in your school, although some of the references in the bibliography may give you useful suggestions.

NOTES

1. Edgar Z. Friedenberg, *Coming of Age in America* (1965).
2. Code of Rights and Responsibilities, National Education Association (1971).

SELECTED BIBLIOGRAPHY AND INFORMATIONAL SOURCES

INTRODUCTION

1. Goldstein, "The Scope and Sources of School Board Authority to Regulate Student Conduct and Status: A Nonconstitutional Analysis," 117 *U. Pa. L. Rev.* 373 (1969).

CHAPTER V
LAW ENFORCEMENT

1. Buss, *Legal Aspects of Crime Investigation in the Public Schools.* A pamphlet published by and available from National Organization on Legal Problems of Education, 825 Western Ave., Topeka, Kansas.
2. Ackerly, *The Reasonable Exercise of Authority.* A pamphlet published by and available from the National Association of Secondary School Principals, 1201 Sixteenth St., N.W., Washington, D.C.

CHAPTER VI
CORPORAL PUNISHMENT

1. "Corporal Punishment in the Public Schools" (1972) ACLU Report, available from ACLU, 20 E. 40th St., New York, N.Y.

2. Citizens Against Physical Punishment, 549 Parkhurst, Dallas, Texas 75218.

3. Report of the Task Force on Corporal Punishment, National Education Association, 1201 16th Street N.W., Washington, D.C. 20036.

CHAPTER VII
DISCRIMINATION

1. The United States Commission on Civil Rights in Washington, D.C. has published a wide variety of reports and studies on the subject of discrimination against minority groups and the poor.

2. *Inequality in Education.* A regular publication of The Center for Law and Education, Larsen Hall, 14 Appian Way, Cambridge, Mass., has devoted parts of several issues to the subject of discrimination.

3. "Need for Studies of Sex Discrimination in Public Schools," a pamphlet available from Citizens' Advisory Council on the Status of Women, Department of Labor Bldg., Room 1336, Washington, D.C. 20210.

4. "Report on Sex Bias in the Public Schools," available from National Organization for Women, 28 E. 56th St., New York, N.Y. 10022.

5. "A Look At Women in Education," a report of the Commissioner's task force of the impact of Office of Education Programs on Women. Department of Health, Education, and Welfare, Office of Education, Washington, D.C. 20202.

Chapter VIII
TRACKING AND CLASSIFICATION

1. Goldberg, et al., *The Effects of Ability Grouping* (1966).
2. Rosenthal & Jacobson, *Pygmalion in the Classroom* (1968).
3. Sexton, *Education and Income* (1962).
4. United States Commission on Civil Rights, "Racial Isolation in the Public Schools" (1967) and many other pamphlets, studies, and reports, available from the Commission in Washington, D.C.
5. Lauter & Howe, "How the School System is Rigged for Failure," *New York Review of Books* (June 18, 1970).
6. Rothstein, *Down the Up Staircase* (1971), a pamphlet available from the Chicago Teacher Center, 852 W. Belmont Ave., Chi., Ill.
7. Schafer, et al., "Programmed for Social Class: Tracking In High School," *Trans-Action* p. 19 (Oct. 1970).
8. *Inequality in Education,* Issues Number 12 and 14, and *Classification Materials,* available from the Center for Law and Education, Larsen Hall, 14 Appian Way, Cambridge, Mass.
9. Findley and Bergen, "Ability Grouping: 1970, Status Impact and Attitudes," available from Center for Educational Improvement, University of Georgia, Athens, Georgia 30601.

CHAPTER X
SCHOOL RECORDS

1. *Guidelines for the Collection, Maintenance and Dissemination of Pupil Records: Report of a Conference on the Ethical and Legal Aspects of School Record Keeping* (1970). A booklet published by and available from the Russell Sage Foundation, 230 Park Avenue, New York, N.Y.)
2. *Code of Student Rights and Responsibilities.* A booklet published by and available from the National Education Assn., 1201 16th St., N.W., Washington, D.C.
3. Butler, *Legal Aspects of Student Records.* A pamphlet published by and available from National Organization on Legal Problems of Education, 825 Western Ave., Topeka, Kansas.

AFTERWORD

SELECTED BIBLIOGRAPHY AND
INFORMATIONAL SOURCES

High School Information Center
1010 Wisconsin Ave. N.W.
Washington, D.C. 20007

"A tax-exempt organization run by high school-aged people which was set up to provide information to high school students who are involved in or concerned about schools, educational reform, student rights, the experiences of other high school activists, and tactics for changing the school system." Write them for their literature list.

Youth Liberation
2007 Washtenaw Avenue
Ann Arbor, Michigan   48104

Provides the following services:
 CHIPS (Cooperative High School Independent Press Syndicate)—provides assistance for students who have started or who want to start independent papers in their schools. Has a directory of papers and a "paper exchange."

 FPS News Service—a tri-weekly news service that provides news and graphics to high school papers (both official and underground).

Write them for their literature list on high school organizing and on other subjects of concern to students.
Teacher Organizing Project (of the New University Conference)
Chicago Teacher Center
852 West Belmont Ave.
Chicago, Illinois   60657

A group of school teachers and education workers searching for better school alternatives, it has written a series of pamphlets "as a theoretical framework for educational alternative" and "to contribute to the growing movement of radical teachers across the country."

Outside the Net
P.O. Box 184
Lansing, Michigan   48901

An education magazine in newspaper form, edited from a radical perspective. It's put out by teachers, students, administrators, and educational researchers; discusses nation-wide concerns in articles, book reviews, poems, comics, etc. 6 issues a year. 50 cents an issue.

New Schools Exchange Newsletter
P.O. Box 820
St. Paris, Ohio 43072

A magazine about free schools, with articles and letters centering about "adult experience and using or living with it." Photographs, book reviews, essays, letters, reports about tactics, etc., contributed by readers and friends. Each month it lists free schools and people, places, conferences, and literature connected with them. Published twice a month. $10 a year.

This Magazine Is About Schools
56 Esplanade St. East, Suite 401
Toronto 215, Ontario

A magazine issued 4 times a year, it began 5 years ago with a strong belief in counter-institutions. Just recently it has shifted emphasis to urban school organizing, with a more socialist and Canadian perspective, yet "the poetic side will continue the search for the details and texture of school experience." In U.S.—$4.00 a year.

Edcentric
2115 "S" Street, N.W.
Washington, D.C. 20008

A magazine that critically examines the conventional schooling system and the movement for educational change, both in the United States and abroad. $5 a year (8 issues).

Student Rights Handbook for New York City
Student Rights Project
New York Civil Liberties Union
84 Fifth Ave.
New York, New York 10011

A pamphlet summarizing the laws and regulations pertaining to student rights in New York City. It can be, and already has been, a useful model for similar handbooks in other parts of the country.

A Student's Book, Wisconsin Coalition for Educational Reform and Wisconsin Student Union
216 N. Hamilton St.
Madison, Wis. 53703

$1 for elementary and secondary school students; $2 for others.

A handbook, still being edited and reworked, "just brimming with helpful hints, hi-jinx, and how-to's on high school organizing"; written to aid the movement "to democratize and humanize our schools."

Lurie, *How to Change the Schools*, Random House (1970).

Strouse, *Up Against The Law*, Signet Books, The New American Library, New York, N.Y. (1970).

A book on the legal rights of people under the age of 21, chapters on student rights, parents, marriage, drugs, sex, driving, employment, contracts, getting busted, the draft.

Glasser and Levine, "Bringing Student Rights to New New York City's School System," 1 *Journal of Law and Education* 213 (1972).

"Student Codes: A Packet on Selected Codes and Related Materials" Center for Law and Education

Larsen Hall, 14 Appian Way
Cambridge, Mass. 02138

"Resist High School Kit"
Resist, Room 4
763 Massachusetts Ave.
Cambridge, Mass. 02139

Contains seven booklets on subjects of concern to students. $2.00 for the kit.

Appendix

A. How To Use This Book

At the end of each chapter, footnotes give references to the decisions of various courts; to the decisions of school officials, to statutes in state law; to the policy of a board of education or a state department of education. These citations will be of use mostly to lawyers, but you may decide to show the actual decision, law, or policy to a school official. A word, then, about how to find the reference.

1. Most court decisions are referred to, or "cited," by the series of volumes in which they appear. For example, the citation for *Tinker* v. *Des Moines Independent Community School District* is 393 U. S. 503 (1969). This means that the case appears in volume 393 of the series called United States Reports, beginning on page 503; the case was decided in 1969. Similarly, "F.2d" or "F.Supp." in a citation refers to another series of volumes in which cases can be found. Again, the numbers refer to the particular volume and page where the decision is printed. The series of volumes containing the decisions can be found in a law library or courthouse in most cities, and a lawyer or law librarian should be able to point you toward the right shelves.

A few court decisions are cited differently, such as *Caldwell* v. *Cannady*, Civil Action No. CA-5-994 (N.D.

Tex. Jan. 27, 1972). Such decisions have not been printed (at least, as of the time that this book was published) and can be obtained by writing the clerk of the court that decided the case (copying costs will generally be charged). The number and date after the name of the case will enable you to identify the case precisely. A lawyer can tell you where to write.

2. Decisions of a commissioner of education can usually be obtained by writing to the commissioner at the department of education in the state capital. Again, the number after the name of the case helps to identify it.

Decisions of the Chancellor or Board of Education of New York City can be obtained by writing to Secretary, Board of Education 110 Livingston Street, Brooklyn, New York 11201.

3. Citations to state laws such as N.H. Rev. State Ann., Title VI, generally refer to volumes available in a law library and sometimes in a lawyer's office.

Policies of a state department of education should be available from the department in the state capital.

Finally a note about how you can use these decisions, laws, or policies. In some instances, they will tell you what the law is in your area and will require that your school follow the same policy. More often, they will indicate what the law is in other areas and what a court might hold to be the law in your area if you went to court. Mostly, you will—or should—use them to try to persuade your school community that since students elsewhere have certain rights, students at your school should have these rights as well.

B. The Tinker Decision (393 U.S. 503 [1969])

SUPREME COURT OF THE UNITED STATES

No. 21—OCTOBER TERM, 1968

| John F. Tinker and Mary Beth Tinker, Minors, etc., et al., Petitioners, v. Des Moines Independent Community School District et al. | On Writ of Certiorari to the United States Court of Appeals for The Eighth Circuit. |

[February 24, 1969.]

MR. JUSTICE FORTAS delivered the opinion of the Court.

Petitioner John F. Tinker, 15 years old, and petitioner Christopher Eckhardt, 16 years old, attended high schools in Des Moines. Petitioner Mary Beth Tinker, John's sister, was a 13-year-old student in junior high school.

In December 1965, a group of adults and students in Des Moines, Iowa, held a meeting at the Eckhardt home. The group determined to publicize their objections to the hostilities in Vietnam and their support for a truce by wearing black armbands during the holiday season and by fasting on December 16 and New Year's Eve. Petitioners and their parents had previously engaged in similar activities, and they decided to participate in the program.

The principals of the Des Moines schools became aware of the plan to wear armbands. On December 14, 1965, they met and adopted a policy that any student wearing an armband to school would be asked to remove it, and if he refused he would be suspended until he returned without the armband. Petitioners were aware of the regulation that the school authorities adopted.

On December 16, Mary Beth and Christopher wore black armbands to their schools. John Tinker wore his armband the next day. They were all sent home and suspended from school until they would come back without their armbands. They did not return to school until after the planned period for wearing armbands had expired—that is, until after New Year's Day.

This complaint was filed in the United States District Court by petitioners, through their fathers, under § 1983 of Title 42 of the United States Code. It prayed for an injunction restraining the defendant school officials and the defendant members of the board of directors of the school district from disciplining the petitioners, and it sought nominal damages. After an evidentiary hearing the District Court dismissed the complaint. It upheld the constitutionality of the school authorities' action on the ground that it was reasonable in order to prevent disturbance of school discipline. 258 F. Supp. 971 (1966). The court referred to but expressly declined to follow the Fifth Circuit's holding in a similar case that prohibition of the wearing of symbols like the armbands cannot be sustained unless it "materially and substantially interfere[s] with the requirements of appropriate discipline in the operation of the school." *Burnside* v. *Byars,* 363 F. 2d 744, 749 (1966).[1]

On appeal, the Court of Appeals for the Eighth Circuit considered the case *en banc.* The court was equally divided, and the District Court's decision was accordingly affirmed, without opinion. 383 F. 2d 988 (1967). We granted certiorari. 390 U. S. 942 (1968).

I

The District Court recognized that the wearing of an armband for the purpose of expressing certain views is

the type of symbolic act that is within the Free Speech
Clause of the First Amendment. See *West Virginia* v.
Barnette, 319 U. S. 624 (1943); *Stromberg* v. *California*,
283 U. S. 359 (1931). Cf. *Thornhill* v. *Alabama*, 310
U. S. 88 (1940); *Edwards* v. *South Carolina*, 372 U. S.
229 (1963); *Brown* v. *Louisiana*, 383 U. S. 131 (1966).
As we shall discuss, the wearing of armbands in the circumstances of this case was entirely divorced from actually or potentially disruptive conduct by those participating
in it. It was closely akin to "pure speech" which, we have
repeatedly held, is entitled to comprehensive protection
under the First Amendment. Compare *Cox* v. *Louisiana*,
379 U. S. 536, 555 (1965); *Adderley* v. *Florida*, 385 U. S.
39 (1966).

First Amendment rights, applied in light of the special
characteristics of the school environment, are available to
teachers and students. It can hardly be argued that either
students or teachers shed their constitutional rights to freedom of speech or expression at the schoolhouse gate. This
has been the unmistakable holding of this Court for almost 50 years. In *Meyer* v. *Nebraska*, 262 U. S. 390
(1923), and *Bartels* v. *Iowa*, 262 U. S. 404 (1923), this
Court, in opinions by Mr. Justice McReynolds, held that
the Due Process Clause of the Fourteenth Amendment
prevents States from forbidding the teaching of a foreign
language to young students. Statutes to this effect, the
Court held, unconstitutionally interfere with the liberty of
teacher, student, and parent.[2] See also *Pierce* v. *Society of
Sisters*, 268 U. S. 510 (1925); *West Virginia* v. *Barnette*,
319 U. S. 624 (1943); *McCollum* v. *Board of Education*,
333 U. S. 203 (1948); *Wieman* v. *Updegraff*, 344 U. S.
183, 195 (1952) (concurring opinion); *Sweezy* v. *New
Hampshire*, 354 U. S. 234 (1957); *Shelton* v. *Tucker*, 364
U. S. 479, 487 (1960); *Engel* v. *Vitale*, 370 U. S. 421

(1962); *Keyishian* v. *Board of Regents*, 385 U. S. 589, 603 (1967); *Epperson* v. *Arkansas*, 393 U. S. 97 (1968).

In *West Virginia* v. *Barnette, supra*, this Court held that under the First Amendment, the student in public school may not be compelled to salute the flag. Speaking through Mr. Justice Jackson, the Court said:

> "The Fourteenth Amendment, as now applied to the States, protects the citizen against the State itself and all of its creatures—Boards of Education not excepted. These have, of course, important, delicate, and highly discretionary functions, but none that they may not perform within the limits of the Bill of Rights. That they are educating the young for citizenship is reason for scrupulous protection of Constitutional freedoms of the individual, if we are not to strangle the free mind at its source and teach youth to discount important principles of our government as mere platitudes." 319 U. S., at 637.

On the other hand, the Court has repeatedly emphasized the need for affirming the comprehensive authority of the States and of school authorities, consistent with fundamental constitutional safeguards, to prescribe and control conduct in the schools. See *Epperson* v. *Arkansas, supra,* at 104; *Meyer* v. *Nebraska, supra,* at 402. Our problem lies in the area where students in the exercise of First Amendment rights collide with the rules of the school authorities.

II.

The problem presented by the present case does not relate to regulation of the length of skirts or the type of clothing, to hair style or deportment. Compare *Ferrell v. Dallas Independent School District,* 392 F. 2d 697 (1968); *Pugsley* v. *Sellmeyer,* 158 Ark. 247, 250 S. W. 538 (1923). It does not concern aggressive, disruptive action or even group demonstrations. Our problem involves direct, primary First Amendment rights akin to "pure speech."

The school officials banned and sought to punish petitioners for a silent, passive, expression of opinion, unaccompanied by any disorder or disturbance on the part of petitioners. There is here no evidence whatever of petitioners' interference, actual or nascent, with the school's work or of collision with the rights of other students to be secure and to be let alone. Accordingly, this case does not concern speech or action that intrudes upon the work of the school or the rights of other students.

Only a few of the 18,000 students in the school system wore the black armbands. Only five students were suspended for wearing them. There is no indication that the work of the school or any class was disrupted. Outside the classrooms, a few students made hostile remarks to the children wearing armbands, but there were no threats or acts of violence on school premises.

The District Court concluded that the action of the school authorities was reasonable because it was based upon their fear of a disturbance from the wearing of the armbands. But, in our system, undifferentiated fear or apprehension of disturbance is not enough to overcome the right to freedom of expression. Any departure from absolute regimentation may cause trouble. Any variation from the majority's opinion may inspire fear. Any word spoken, in class, in the lunchroom or on the campus, that deviates from the views of another person, may start an argument or cause a disturbance. But our Constitution says we must take this risk. *Terminiello* v. *Chicago,* 337 U. S. 1. (1959); and our history says that it is this sort of hazardous freedom—this kind of openness—that is the basis of our National strength and of the independence and vigor of Americans who grow up and live in this relatively permissive, often disputatious society.

In order for the State in the person of school officials to justify prohibition of a particular expression of opinion, it must be able to show that its action was caused by something more than a mere desire to avoid the discomfort and unpleasantness that always accompany an unpopular viewpoint. Certainly where there is no finding and no showing that the exercise of the forbidden right would "materially and substantially interfere with the requirements of appropriate discipline in the operation of the school," the prohibition cannot be sustained. *Burnside v. Byars, supra,* at 749.

In the present case, the District Court made no such finding, and our independent examination of the record fails to yield evidence that the school authorities had reason to anticipate that the wearing of the armbands would substantially interfere with the work of the school or impinge upon the rights of other students. Even an official memorandum prepared after the suspension that listed the reasons for the ban on wearing the armbands made no reference to the anticipation of such disruption.[8]

On the contrary, the action of the school authorities appears to have been based upon an urgent wish to avoid the controversy which might result from the expression, even by the silent symbol of armbands, of opposition to this Nation's part in the conflagration in Vietnam.[4] It is revealing, in this respect, that the meeting at which the school principals decided to issue the contested regulation was called in response to a student's statement to the journalism teacher in one of the schools that he wanted to write an article on Vietnam and have it published in the school paper. (The student was dissuaded.)[5]

It is also relevant that the school authorities did not purport to prohibit the wearing of all symbols of political or controversial significance. The record shows that students in some of the schools wore buttons relating to national political campaigns, and some even wore the Iron Cross, traditionally a symbol of nazism. The order prohibiting the wearing of armbands did not extend to these. Instead, a particular symbol—black armbands worn to exhibit opposition to this Nation's involvement in Vietnam—was singled out for prohibition. Clearly, the prohibition of expression of one particular opinion, at least without evidence that it is necessary to avoid material and substantial interference with school work or discipline, is not constitutionally permissible.

In our system, state-operated schools may not be enclaves of totalitarianism. School officials do not possess absolute authority over their students. Students in school as well as out of school are "persons" under our Constitution. They are possessed of fundamental rights which the State must respect, just as they themselves must respect their obligations to the State. In our system, students may not be regarded as closed-circuit recipients of only that which the State chooses to communicate. They may not be confined to the expression of those sentiments that are officially approved. In the absence of a specific showing of constitutionally valid reasons to regulate their speech, students are entitled to freedom of expression of their views. As Judge Gewin, speaking for the Fifth Circuit said, school officials cannot suppress "expressions of feelings with which they do not wish to contend." *Burnside v. Byars, supra,* at 749.

In *Meyer* v. *Nebraska, supra,* at 402, Justice McReynolds expressed this Nation's repudiation of the principle that a State might so conduct its schools as to "foster a homogeneous people." He said:

> "In order to submerge the individual and develop ideal citizens, Sparta assembled the males at seven into barracks and intrusted their subsequent education and training to official guardians. Although such measures have been deliberately approved by men of great genius, their ideas touching the relation between individual and State were wholly different from those upon which our institutions rest; and it hardly will be affirmed that any legislature could impose such restrictions upon the people of a State without doing violence to both letter and spirit of the Constitution."

This principle has been repeated by this Court on numerous occasions during the intervening years. In *Keyishian* v. *Board of Regents,* 385 U. S. 589, 603, MR. JUSTICE BRENNAN, speaking for the Court, said:

> " 'The vigilant protection of constitutional freedom is nowhere more vital than in the community of American schools.' *Shelton* v. *Tucker,* 234 U. S. 479, 487. The classroom is peculiarly the 'market-place of ideas.' The Nation's future depends upon leaders trained through wide exposure to that robust exchange of ideas which discovers truth 'out of a multitude of tongues, [rather] than through any kind of authoritative selection'. . . ."

The principle of these cases is not confined to the supervised and ordained discussion which takes place in the classroom. The principal use to which the schools are dedicated is to accommodate students during prescribed hours for the purpose of certain types of activities. Among those activities is personal intercommunication among the students.[6] This is not only an inevitable part of the process of attending school. It is also an important part of the educational process. A student's rights therefore, do not embrace merely the classroom hours. When he is in the cafeteria, or on the playing field, or on the campus during the authorized hours, he may express his opinions, even on controversial subjects like the conflict in Vietnam, if he does so "without materially and substantially interfering with appropriate discipline in the operation of the school" and without colliding with the rights of others. *Burnside* v. *Byars, supra,* at 749. But conduct by the student, in class or out of it, which for any reason— whether it stems from time, place, or type of behavior— materially disrupts classwork or involves substantial disorder or invasion of the rights of others is, of course, not immunized by the constitutional guaranty of freedom of speech. Cf. *Blackwell* v. *Issaquena City Bd. of Educ.,* 303 F. 2d 749 (C. A. 5th Cir., 1966).

Under our Constitution, free speech is not a right that is given only to be so circumscribed that it exists in principle but not in fact. Freedom of expression would not truly exist if the right could be exercised only in an area that a benevolent government has provided as a safe haven for crackpots. The Constitution says that Congress (and the States) may not abridge the right to free speech. This provision means what it says. We properly read it to permit reasonable regulation of speech-connected activities in carefully restricted circumstances. But we do not confine the permissible exercise of First Amendment rights to a telephone booth or the four corners of a pamphlet, or to supervised and ordained discussion in a school classroom.

If a regulation were adopted by school officials forbidding discussion of the Vietnam conflict, or the expression by any student of opposition to it anywhere on
school property except as part of a prescribed classroom
exercise, it would be obvious that the regulation would
violate the constitutional rights of students, at least if it
could not be justified by a showing that the students' activities would materially and substantially disrupt the work
and discipline of the school. Cf. *Hammond* v. *South Carolina State College,* 272 F. Supp. 947 (D. C. D. S. C. 1967)
(orderly protest meeting on state college campus); *Dickey*
v. *Alabama State Board,* 273 F. Supp. 613 (D. C. M. D.
Ala. 1967) (expulsion of student editor of college newspaper). In the circumstances of the present case, the prohibition of the silent, passive "witness of the armbands," as
one of the children called it, is no less offensive to the Constitution's guaranties.

As we have discussed, the record does not demonstrate
any facts which might reasonably have led school authorities to forecast substantial disruption of or material
interference with school activities, and no disturbances or
disorders on the school premises in fact occurred. These
petitioners merely went about their ordained rounds in
school. Their deviation consisted only in wearing on their
sleeve a band of black cloth, not more than two inches
wide. They wore it to exhibit their disapproval of the Vietnam hostilities and their advocacy of a truce, to make their
views known, and by their example, to influence others to
adopt them. They neither interrupted school activities nor
sought to intrude in the school affairs or the lives of others.
They caused discussion outside of the class rooms, but
no interference with work and no disorder. In the circum-

stances, our Constitution does not permit officials of the State to deny their form of expression.

We express no opinion as to the form of relief which should be granted, this being a matter for the lower courts to determine. We reverse and remand for further proceedings consistent with this opinion.

Reversed and remanded.

NOTES

[1]In *Burnside*, the Fifth Circuit ordered that high school authorities be enjoined from enforcing a regulation forbidding students to wear "freedom buttons." It is instructive that in *Blackwell* v. *Issaquena County Board of Education*, 363 F. 2d 749 (1966), the same panel on the same day reached the opposite result on different facts. It declined to enjoin enforcement of such a regulation in another high school where the students wearing freedom buttons harassed students who did not wear them and created much disturbance.

[2]*Hamilton* v. *Regents of Univ. of Cal.*, 293 U.S. 245 (1934) is sometimes cited for the broad proposition that the State may attach conditions to attendance at a state university that require individuals to violate their religious convictions. The case involved dismissal of members of a religious denomination from a land grant college for refusal to participate in military training. Narrowly viewed, the case turns upon the Court's conclusion that merely requiring a student to participate in school training in military "science" could not conflict with his constitutionally protected freedom of conscience. The decision cannot be taken as establishing that the State may impose and enforce any conditions that it chooses upon attendance at public institutions of learning, however violative they may be of fundamental constitutional guaranties. See, *e. g.*, *West Virginia* v. *Barnette*, 319 U.S. 624 (1943); *Dixon* v. *Alabama State Bd. of Educ.*, 294 F. 2d 150 (C. A. 5th Cir. 1961); *Knight* v. *State Bd. of Educ.*, 200 F. Supp. 174 (D.C.M.D. Tenn. 1961); *Dickey* v. *Alabama St. Bd. of Educ.*, 273 F. Supp. 613 (C.A.M.D. Ala. 1967). See also Note, 73 Harv. L. Rev. 1595 (1960); Note, 81 Harv. L. Rev. 1045 (1968).

[3]The only suggestions of fear of disorder in the report are these: "A former student of one of our high schools was killed in Viet Nam. Some of his friends are still in school and it was

felt that if any kind of a demonstration existed, it might evolve
into something which would be difficult to control.

"Students at one of the high schools were heard to say they
would wear arm bands of other colors if the black bands
prevailed."

Moreover, the testimony of school authorities at trial indicates
that it was not fear of disruption that motivated the regulation
prohibiting the armbands; the regulation was directed against
"the principle of the demonstration" itself. School authorities
simply felt that "the schools are no place for demonstrations,"
and if the students "didn't like the way our elected officials
were handling things, it should be handled with the ballot box
and not in the halls of our public schools."

⁴The District Court found that the school authorities, in
prohibiting black armbands, were influenced by the fact that
"[t]he Viet Nam war and the involvement of the United States
therein has been the subject of a major controversy for some
time. When the armband regulation involved herein was
promulgated, debate over the Viet Nam war had become
vehement in many localities. A protest march against the war
had been recently held in Washington, D.C. A wave of draft-
card-burning incidents protesting the war had swept the country.
At that time two highly publicized draft card burning cases
were pending in this Court. Both individuals supporting the war
and those opposing it were quite vocal in expressing their
views." 258 F. Supp. at 972–973.

⁵After the principals' meeting, the director of secondary
education and the principal of the high school informed the
student that the principals were opposed to publication of his
article. They reported that "we felt that it was a very friendly
conversation, although we did not feel that we had convinced
the student that our decision was a just one."

⁶In *Hammond* v. *South Carolina State College*, 272 F. Supp.
947 (D.C.D.S.C. 1967), District Judge Hemphill had before
him a case involving a meeting on campus of 300 students to
express their views on school practices. He pointed out that
a school is not like a hospital or a jail enclosure. Cf. *Cox v.
Louisiana*, 379 U.S. 536 (1965); *Adderley* v. *Florida*, 385 U.S.
39 (1966). It is a public place, and its dedication to specific
uses does not imply that the constitutional rights of persons
entitled to be there are to be gauged as if the premises were
purely private property. Cf. *Edwards* v. *South Carolina*, 372
U.S. 229 (1963); *Brown* v. *Louisiana*, 383 U.S. 131 (1966).